JOURNEYS

Reader's Notebook
Volume 2

Grade 2

 HOUGHTON MIFFLIN HARCOURT
School Publishers

Printed in the U.S.A.

ISBN   978-0-547-86063-3

26 27 28 29 30   0982   21 20 19 18 17

4500656881   C D E F G

Contents

Base Words and Endings
-ed, -ing

Add -ing or -ed to each base word to make a new word.
Double the final consonant if you need to. Say the word.
Then write the number of syllables you hear.

1. bag + ing = _____ ___

2. help + ed = _____ ___

3. swim + ing = _____ ___

4. rub + ed = _____ ___

5. trot + ed = _____ ___

Read the sentence. Underline the word that ends with -ing
or -ed. Then write the base word on the line.

6. Maria played baseball with her pals. _____

7. She batted last on her team. _____

8. She was fast at running the bases. _____

9. Sometimes she missed the ball. _____

10. Maria wanted to be a good player. _____

Naming with Pronouns

The subject of a sentence names the person or thing that does the action of the verb. A **pronoun** can take the place of this noun.

<u>Greg</u> is sick at home.	**Subject** Greg
<u>He</u> is sick at home.	**Pronoun** He

Thinking Question
Which pronoun can take the place of the noun or nouns in the subject?

Write the pronoun that can take the place of the underlined subject. Use the words in the box to help you.

He	She	It	They

1. <u>Lisa</u> has an idea.

_____

2. <u>The students</u> make a card.

_____

3. <u>Ben</u> puts the card in the mailbox.

_____

4. <u>The card</u> makes Greg smile.

_____

5. <u>Greg</u> puts his card on his desk.

_____

Base Words and Endings
-ed, -ing

Underline each base word. Then write each word in the
correct column.

```
···············  Word Bank  ···············

    fanning     flipped      dotted     dropping
    wagged      pumping      jumped     planned
    rented      begging      patted     melted
```

-ed words 1 syllable	-ed words 2 syllables	-ing words 2 syllables
1. _____	5. _____	9. _____
2. _____	6. _____	10. _____
3. _____	7. _____	11. _____
4. _____	8. _____	12. _____

Choose two words from above. Change the ending from -ed
to -ing or from -ing to -ed. Write a sentence for each word.

13. _____

_____

14. _____

_____

Base Words with Endings -*ed*, -*ing*

Sort the Spelling Words that end in -*ed* and -*ing*.

Words that end in -*ed*	Words that end in -*ing*
1. _____	9. _____
2. _____	10. _____
3. _____	11. _____
4. _____	12. _____
5. _____	13. _____
6. _____	14. _____
7. _____	
8. _____	

Spelling Words

Basic Words

1. running
2. clapped
3. stopped
4. hopping
5. batted
6. selling
7. pinned
8. cutting
9. sitting
10. rubbed
11. missed
12. grabbed

Review Words

13. mixed
14. going

Write four Basic Words in which you double the final consonant when adding -*ed* or -*ing*.

15. _____

16. _____

17. _____

18. _____

Using Pronouns

- Use a **pronoun** to replace a noun that comes after a verb.
- Use these pronouns: *me, him, her, it, us*, and *them*.

Nouns	Pronouns
Bob rides a <u>bike</u>.	Bob rides **it.**
I saw <u>Bob</u> in the park.	I saw **him** in the park.
He saw <u>my friends</u>.	He saw **them.**
He talked to <u>Tanya and me</u>.	He talked to **us.**

Thinking Question
Which pronoun can take the place of the noun or nouns after the verb?

Draw a line under the pronoun in ( ) that should take the place of the underlined noun. Write the new sentence.

1. The artist talks to <u>his customers</u>. (them, me)

_____

2. A customer gives <u>Anthony</u> money. (her, him)

_____

3. The artist sells <u>a painting</u>. (it, us)

_____

4. Trisha laughs at <u>Gina and me</u>. (her, us)

_____

Focus Trait: Ideas
Details

Without Details	With Details
He looked at the people.	He looked **out the window** at the **crowd of people shouting and waving.**

A. Read these sentences about *Mr. Tanen's Tie Trouble*.
Add details to help readers see what is happening.

Without Details	With Details
1. Mr. Tanen was upset.	Mr. Tanen was upset _____ _____
2. Everyone came.	Everyone came _____ _____

B. Read each sentence. Look at the picture on pages 24–25 of
Mr. Tanen's Tie Trouble. Add your own details to make each
sentence more interesting. Write your new sentences.

Without Details	With Details
3. Mr. Tanen held up a tie.	
4. The dentist bought a tie.	
5. The ties were nice.	

Cumulative Review

Complete each sentence with a long *o* word from the box.

Word Bank

float	boat	blow	slow
cold	go	soaked	

1. Sam sailed his _____ on the pond.

2. A strong wind can _____ a sailboat across the lake.

3. Turtles are _____ animals.

4. The rocks did not _____ in the water.

5. We got _____ on a rainy day.

6. We felt _____ after playing outside in the snow.

7. Cars _____ when the light turns green.

Now use one of the long *o* words in a sentence.

8. _____

_____

Reader's Guide

Mr. Tanen's Tie Trouble

Draw a Tie

Hi. I'm Mr. Tanen. I love ties, but I learned that I love something else even more. Use details from the story to show what I learned.

Read page 16. What does Mr. Tanen love?

_____

_____

Read pages 18–19. What makes Mr. Tanen so happy?

_____

_____

_____

Read pages 26–27. Why can't Mr. Tanen sell his Blue Ribbon tie?

_____

_____

Read pages 30–32. How does Mr. Tanen feel about the playground?

_____

_____

Mr. Tanen wants to have a tie made to remember the special day when the playground opened. Use details from the story to create the tie. Write a sentence to tell about the tie you made for Mr. Tanen.

_____

_____

Name _____ Date _____

Lesson 16
READER'S NOTEBOOK

Mr. Tanen's Tie Trouble
Spelling: Base Words with
Endings -ed, -ing

Base Words with Endings -ed, -ing

Write the base word of each Spelling Word.

1. pinned _____

2. rubbed _____

3. missed _____

4. batted _____

5. mixed _____

6. going _____

Write the Basic Word that belongs with each pair of words.

7. jogging, skipping _____

8. buying, paying _____

9. took, pulled _____

10. cheered, applauded _____

11. ripping, trimming _____

12. jumping, leaping _____

13. halted, ended _____

14. resting, sleeping _____

Spelling Words

Basic Words

1. running
2. clapped
3. stopped
4. hopping
5. batted
6. selling
7. pinned
8. cutting
9. sitting
10. rubbed
11. missed
12. grabbed

Review Words

13. mixed
14. going

Naming Yourself Last

Rewrite each sentence correctly.

1. I and Ann had a picnic by myself.

_____

2. When do she and i need to come in?

_____

3. Yesterday, i played at home by ourselves.

_____

Underline the pronoun that can take the place of the underlined noun or nouns. Then write the new sentence.

4. The team captain picked <u>Caitlin and Eric.</u> (them, we)

_____

5. The coach helped <u>Molly.</u> (she, her)

_____

6. The tall kid hit <u>the ball.</u> (them, it)

_____

Homographs

Look for words in the sentence that show the meaning of the underlined word. Circle one or more clue words in each sentence. Then circle the correct meaning below the sentence.

1. I gave my mom a <u>present</u> for her birthday.

   gift   not absent

2. Does your baby brother ever <u>rest</u>?

   what is left   go to sleep

3. Are you a <u>pupil</u> in my class?

   student   part of the eye

4. Make a <u>ring</u> around your answer.

   circle   sound of a bell   jewelry for a finger

5. Please take this <u>slip</u> to the office.

   small piece of paper   slide easily

6. Please wait a <u>second</u> and I will answer your question.

   right after the first   part of a minute

Proofread for Spelling

Proofread the paragraph. Circle the eight misspelled
words. Then write the correct spellings on the
lines below.

When my sister went away to school, her cat
mised her. Kitty stoped eating. She started runing in
circles. I didn't know what to do. I claped my hands and
called her name. I tried hoping around. I bated balls
to her. Nothing made her feel better! Finally, I had an
idea. I grabed some of my sister's clothes and put them
in Kitty's bed. Kitty rubed against the clothes. Then she
curled up and started purring!

Spelling Words

**Basic
Words**
1. running
2. clapped
3. stopped
4. hopping
5. batted
6. selling
7. pinned
8. cutting
9. sitting
10. rubbed
11. missed
12. grabbed

1. _____   5. _____

2. _____   6. _____

3. _____   7. _____

4. _____   8. _____

Put the parts of each word in order. Then write the Spelling
Word correctly.

9. nedpin _____

10. lingsel _____

11. ttuingc _____

12. tingsit _____

Kinds of Sentences

Write whether the sentence is a statement, command, or question. Write the sentence correctly on the line.

1. where is the bake sale _____

_____

2. hang this sign _____

_____

3. the money helps the school _____

_____

4. do you like cookies _____

_____

5. share with your sister. _____

_____

6. I like cookies with green icing _____

_____

Sentence Fluency

Sentences with Repeated Subjects	Better Sentences
Tony walks to the store. <u>Tony</u> buys milk and eggs.	Tony walks to the store. **He** buys milk and eggs.

Sentences with Repeated Subjects	Better Sentences
Mr. Shay and Mrs. Shay need help shopping. <u>Mr. Shay and Mrs. Shay</u> cannot go to the store.	Mr. Shay and Mrs. Shay need help shopping. **They** cannot go the store.

Use a pronoun to replace the subject in the underlined sentence. Write the new sentence.

1. Tony likes to help the Shays. <u>Tony goes to their house each day.</u>

   _____

2. Mrs. Shay likes Tony. <u>Mrs. Shay makes lunch for Tony.</u>

   _____

3. Tony and Mr. Shay sit on the porch. <u>Tony and Mr. Shay play chess.</u>

   _____

4. Tony goes to the store. <u>The store sells good food.</u>

   _____

Long *i* (*i, igh, ie, y*)

Write a word from the box to complete each sentence.

> **Word Bank**
>
> might   pie   kind
> find   night   My

1. Do you like _____ made with fruit?

2. What _____ of pie do you like best?

3. _____ mom will go to the store to get fresh peaches.

4. I _____ go with her.

5. We will _____ the best peaches together.

6. At _____ we will eat peach pie.

Subjects and Verbs

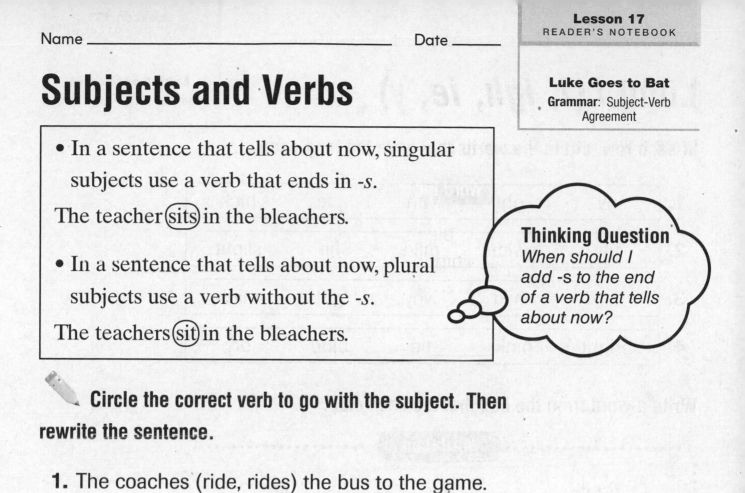

- In a sentence that tells about now, singular subjects use a verb that ends in *-s*.

The teacher (sits) in the bleachers.

- In a sentence that tells about now, plural subjects use a verb without the *-s*.

The teachers (sit) in the bleachers.

Thinking Question
When should I add -s to the end of a verb that tells about now?

Circle the correct verb to go with the subject. Then rewrite the sentence.

1. The coaches (ride, rides) the bus to the game.

_____

2. My friend (hand, hands) the man a ticket.

_____

3. Mom and Dad (cheer, cheers) at the game.

_____

4. The players (look, looks) at the goalie.

_____

5. The kicker (kick, kicks) the ball.

_____

Long *i* (*i*, *igh*, *ie*, *y*)

In each row, circle the words that have the long *i* sound.

1.	by	light	win	pie	pick

2.	ply	swim	mild	fin	slight

3.	milk	child	why	gift	thigh

4.	bright	pink	tie	bind	dry

Write a word from the box that fits each clue.

Word Bank

right   fly   tie
cry   kind

5. This is what a jet does. _____

6. You do this with laces. _____

7. A nice pal is this. _____

8. If you don't go left, you might go this way.

_____

9. A child might do this when he or she is sad.

_____

Long *i* (*i*, *igh*, *y*)

Sort the Spelling Words. Put words with the long *i* sound spelled *i*, *igh*, and *y* under the correct baseball glove.

Spelling Words
Basic Words
1. night
2. kind
3. spy
4. child
5. light
6. find
7. right
8. high
9. wild
10. July
11. fry
12. sigh
Review Words
13. by
14. why

i	*igh*	*y*
1. _____	5. _____	10. _____
2. _____	6. _____	11. _____
3. _____	7. _____	12. _____
4. _____	8. _____	13. _____
	9. _____	14. _____

Circle the letter or letters in each word that spell the long *i* sound.

Subjects and More Verbs

In a sentence that tells about now, add *-es* to a verb that ends in *s, sh, ch, tch, z,* or *x* to match a singular subject.

Thinking Question
When should I add -es to the end of a verb that tells about now?

The trains pass the rink.   The train passes the rink.

The girls watch the skaters.   The girl watches the skaters.

The chefs mix hot soup.   The chef mixes hot soup.

The boys reach for a ball.   The boy reaches for a ball.

Draw a line under each correct sentence.

1. The coach fix the skates.

The coach fixes the skates.

2. The kids dash around the rink.

The kids dashes around the rink.

3. The teacher teaches them a trick.

The teacher teach them a trick.

4. Dad misses a turn.

Dad miss a turn.

5. Mom watch from the stands.

Mom watches from the stands.

Focus Trait: Voice
Using Dialogue

Without Dialogue	With Dialogue
Dani wanted to go to the baseball game.	Dani begged, "Mom, please let me go to the baseball game. Please!"

A. Rewrite each sentence. Use dialogue.

Without Dialogue	With Dialogue
1. Dani asked Mom about the score.	"_____?" Dani asked Mom.
2. Mom told her it was tied.	"_____," Mom said.

B. Rewrite each sentence. Use dialogue.

Sentence	Dialogue
3. Tad told Dani she couldn't play.	
4. Dani wanted to know why.	
5. Tad said she was too young.	

Cumulative Review

Combine a word from the box with a word below. Write the word on the line, and read the whole compound word.

Word Bank

be	box	hive
cake	boat	ball
end	light	

1. pan _____

2. sun _____

3. bee _____

4. base _____

5. may _____

6. week _____

7. sand _____

8. sail _____

Circle two compound words in each sentence. Draw a line between the two words that make up each compound word.

9. We like to look for pinecones in the sunshine.

10. She put on her raincoat and went outside.

Reader's Guide

Luke Goes to Bat

Luke's Game-Day Journal

A journal lets you tell what happens in your day and share your feelings. Finish Luke's journal, using ideas from the text.

Read pages 54–55. Imagine you are Luke. Write in Luke's journal about this day.

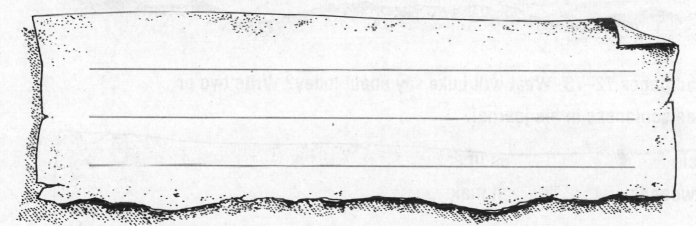

Read pages 58–60. Imagine you are Luke. Write in Luke's journal about this day.

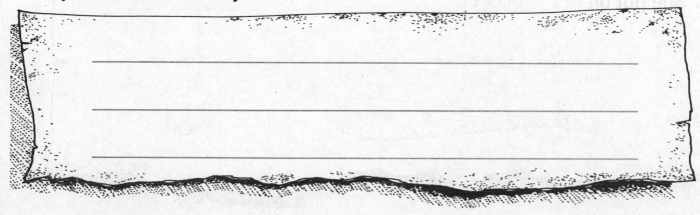

Read pages 63–65. What is important about this day?
Write two or three sentences in Luke's journal.

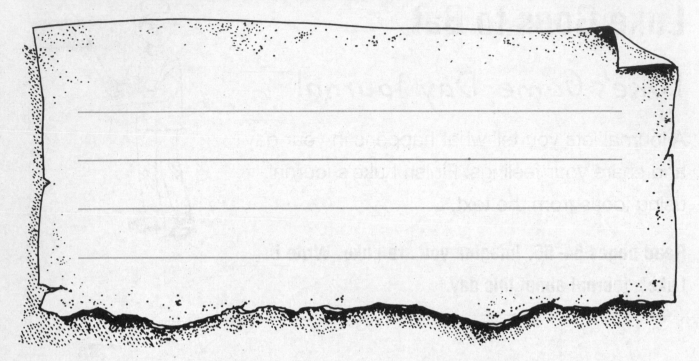

_____

_____

_____

_____

Read pages 72–73. What will Luke say about today? Write two or
three sentences in his journal.

_____

_____

_____

_____

Long *i* (*i, igh, y*)

Write a Spelling Word for each clue.

1. This is a month of the year. _____

2. You can cook food this way. _____

3. This also means *correct*. _____

4. The opposite of *tame* _____

5. A young person _____

6. A word that asks a question _____

7. When the sky is dark _____

8. A word that can mean *next to* _____

Add and subtract letters from the words below to write Spelling Words.

9. (spray – ra) = _____

10. (bright – br) + l = _____

11. (signal – nal) + h = _____

12. (fight – ght) + nd = _____

Spelling Words
Basic Words
1. night
2. kind
3. spy
4. child
5. light
6. find
7. right
8. high
9. wild
10. July
11. fry
12. sigh
Review
13. by
14. why

Pronouns and Verbs

- If the pronoun *he, she,* or *it* is the subject of a sentence that tells about now, add *–s* or *–es* to the verb.

He throws the ball. She catches the ball.

- If the pronoun *I, you, we,* or *they* is the subject of a sentence that tells about now, do not add *–s* or *–es* to the verb.

They watch the game. We cheer very loudly.

✏️ **Circle the correct verb to match the subject. Then write the sentence.**

1. We (climb, climbs) to our seats.

_____

2. She (hand, hands) programs to people.

_____

3. I (reach, reaches) for one.

_____

4. You (look, looks) cold.

_____

5. He (fix, fixes) a snack.

_____

26

Antonyms

Draw a line from each word on the left to its antonym on the right.

find   whispered

below   above

yelled   lose

final   beginning

Read each sentence. Think of a word that has the opposite meaning of the underlined word and write it on the line.

1. Emily had to <u>find</u> her library book.

_____

2. After the game, the <u>final</u> score was six to three.

_____

3. We <u>yelled</u> when the parade came down the street.

_____

4. You can't ride if your head is <u>below</u> the line.

_____

Proofread for Spelling

**Proofread the journal entry. Circle the misspelled words.
Then write the correct spellings on the lines below.**

   Last knight, I was so afraid. I heard a wilde
scream from somewhere outside. I tried to turn on
the lite, but it was up too hi. It was so cold. It seemed
more like January than Julli. I didn't know what to do.
I let out a sye and went to sleep.

1. _____   4. _____

2. _____   5. _____

3. _____   6. _____

**Find and circle six Spelling Words with long *i*. The words
can read across or down.**

Q	L	W	M	X	P	F	R	Y
F	I	N	D	G	R	T	Z	P
K	D	B	X	R	O	V	M	W
I	X	C	H	I	L	D	N	I
N	V	J	S	G	R	K	N	L
D	M	P	A	H	K	N	E	D
Q	A	M	F	T	U	V	A	R

Spelling Words
Basic Words
1. night
2. kind
3. spy
4. child
5. light
6. find
7. right
8. high
9. wild
10. July
11. fry
12. sigh

Kinds of Sentences

Read each sentence. Tell whether it is a statement, an exclamation, a command, or a question. Then write the sentence correctly on the line.

1. did you hit that ball _____

_____

2. you did a great job _____

_____

3. try that again _____

_____

4. Hanna pitches the ball _____

_____

5. her dad hits the ball _____

_____

6. how far did he hit it _____

_____

Subjects and Verbs

Subject and Verb Don't Match	Subject and Verb Match
Jared <u>pitch</u> the ball.	Jared <u>pitches</u> the ball.
She <u>swing</u> the bat.	She <u>swings</u> the bat.

Proofread the paragraphs. Find five places where the subject and verb do not match. Write the corrected sentences on the lines below.

Mike play baseball with me. He pitches the ball.
I hit the ball. It get dark out. Mom call me. She yells,
"Dinner!"

I wave at Mike. He wave back. He rush home, too.

1. _____

2. _____

3. _____

4. _____

5. _____

Long *e* Sound for *y*

Circle the word that tells about each picture. Then use the words to complete the sentences below.

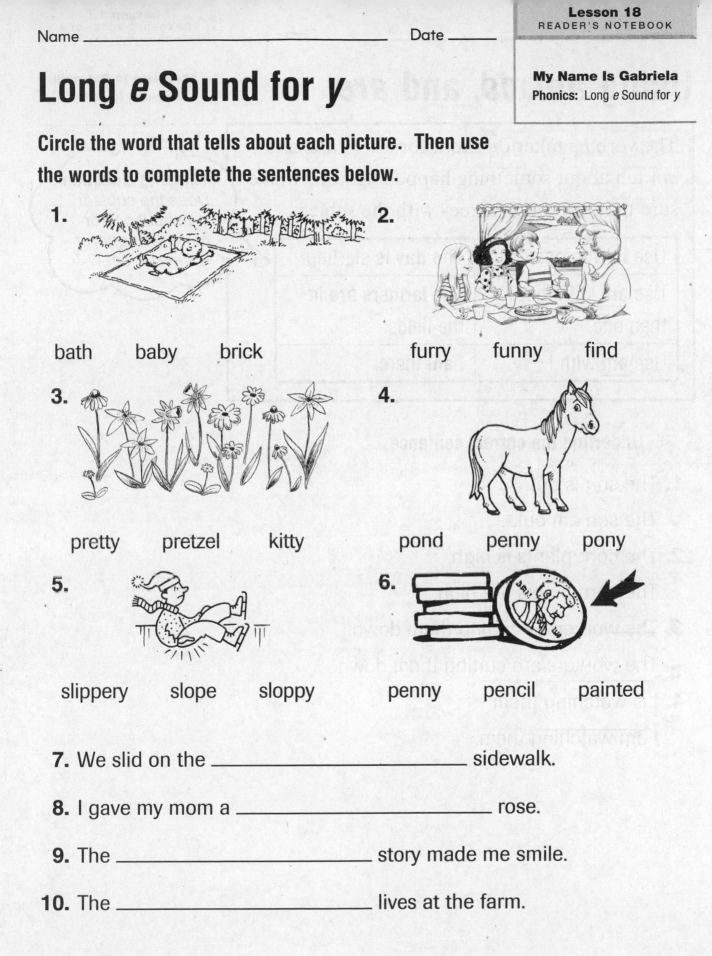

1. bath   baby   brick

2. furry   funny   find

3. pretty   pretzel   kitty

4. pond   penny   pony

5. slippery   slope   sloppy

6. penny   pencil   painted

7. We slid on the _____ sidewalk.

8. I gave my mom a _____ rose.

9. The _____ story made me smile.

10. The _____ lives at the farm.

Using *am*, *is*, and *are*

The verb *be* takes different forms. *Is, are,* and *am* tell about something happening now. Make sure the form of *be* agrees with the subject.

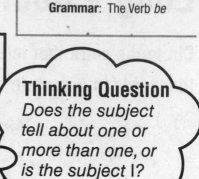

Thinking Question
Does the subject tell about one or more than one, or is the subject I?

Use **is** with one.	**The day is** starting.
Use **are** with more than one.	**The farmers are** in the fields.
Use **am** with I.	**I am** there.

✏️ **Underline the correct sentence.**

1. The sun is out.

The sun am out.

2. The corn plants is high.

The corn plants are high.

3. The workers is cutting them down.

The workers are cutting them down.

4. I is watching them.

I am watching them.

Name _____ Date _____

Long *e* Sound for *y*

**Choose a word from the box to complete each sentence.
Write it on the line.**

Word Bank

funny	tiny	lady	many
sunny	muddy	puppy	happy

1. Today is a hot, _____ day.

2. My baby sister is _____.

3. Wipe your _____ feet before
you come in.

4. Do you want to hear a _____
joke?

5. A _____ in the store helped
me find a gift for Mom.

6. How _____ children are in
our class?

7. I always feel _____ when
I sing.

8. My _____ likes to bark at
the moon.

Long *e* Spelled *y*

Write the Basic Words with double consonants in one list.
Write the words with single consonants in another list.

Spelling Words

Double Consonants   **Single Consonants**

1. _____   8. _____

2. _____   9. _____

3. _____   10. _____

4. _____   11. _____

5. _____   12. _____

6. _____

7. _____

Basic Words
1. happy
2. pretty
3. baby
4. very
5. puppy
6. funny
7. carry
8. lucky
9. only
10. sunny
11. penny
12. city

Review Words
13. tiny
14. many

Using *was* and *were*

The verb **be** takes different forms. **Was** and **were** tell about something that happened in the past. Make sure the form of **be** agrees with the subject.

Use **was** with one.	The **market was** busy.
Use **were** with more than one.	**Papa and Emelina were** shopping.

Thinking Question
Does the subject tell about one or more than one, or is the subject I?

✏ **Write each sentence correctly.**

1. Mama (was, were) cooking.

_____

2. The beans (was, were) boiling.

_____

3. The rice (was, were) done.

_____

4. We (was, were) hungry.

_____

Focus Trait: Word Choice Using Sense Words

Without Sense Words	With Sense Words
I took off my glove and touched the snow.	I took off my glove and touched the <u>cold</u>, <u>white</u> snow.

Read each description. Use sense words to fill in the blanks.

Without Sense Words	With Sense Words
1. I drank some juice.	I drank some juice that tasted like _____.
2. The barn was filled with pigs.	The barn was filled with _____ pigs.

Pair/Share Work with a partner to add sense words.

Without Sense Words	With Sense Words
3. I saw a field.	
4. She laughed.	
5. I ate a pickle.	

Changing *y* to *i*

Read the word. Then change *y* to *i* and add *es* to make the word mean more than one. Write the new word.

1.

pony

_____

2.

puppy

_____

3.

baby

_____

Write two sentences with the words that you wrote.

4. _____

5. _____

Reader's Guide

My Name Is Gabriela

Make an Invitation

Garbriela Mistral is a famous writer who won an award
for her writing. Gather some details about her life.

**Read pages 92–95. Does Gabriela Mistral have a good
imagination? How can you tell?**

_____

_____

_____

**Read pages 100–101. Gabriela Mistral liked to play school.
Do you think she was a good pretend teacher? How can you tell?**

_____

_____

**Read pages 103 and 107. Did Gabriela Mistral still have a
good imagination after she grew up? How can you tell?**

_____

_____

Imagine you are having a party for Gabriela Mistral. Use what you learned about Gabriela's life to finish the invitation. Make an illustration showing something from Gabriela's imagination.

Who: Gabriela Mistral

What: A Celebration of Gabriela's Nobel Prize

Where: Gabriela's family home in Elqui Valley

When: Saturday at 2:00

Read pages 104–106. Say what you think Gabriela will tell her friends about her life.

Gabriela will give a short talk. She will tell us about

_____

_____

Think about what you learned about Gabriela Mistral. What would she want for the schools?

Instead of a gift for Gabriela, please bring a gift for the local school. Bring: _____

_____

Draw a picture from Gabriela's imagination.

Long *e* Spelled *y*

Write a Basic Word that has the same or almost the same meaning for each word.

Spelling Words

Basic Words

1. happy
2. pretty
3. baby
4. very
5. puppy
6. funny
7. carry
8. lucky
9. only
10. sunny
11. penny
12. city

Review Words

13. tiny
14. many

1. beautiful _____

2. dog _____

3. hold _____

4. infant _____

5. silly _____

6. coin _____

Write a Basic Word to complete each sentence.

7. In the summer, the sky is often _____.

8. When I smile, it is because I am _____.

9. I think I am _____ because I often win.

10. I would like to live in a big _____.

11. Ms. Carter was _____ pleased with our reports.

12. My little sister has _____ one front tooth.

Name _____   Date _____

Using *Being* Verbs

Underline the correct sentence.

1. The rodeo is here.

The rodeo are here.

The rodeo am here.

2. The crowds is clapping.

The crowds are clapping.

The crowds am clapping.

Write each sentence correctly.

3. Gabriela (was, were) a teacher.

_____

4. She (was, were) speaking.

_____

5. Her students (was, were) listening.

_____

6. They (was, were) learning a lot.

_____

Name _____   Date _____

Lesson 18
READER'S NOTEBOOK

My Name Is Gabriela
Vocabulary Strategies:
Suffixes -*y* and -*ful*

Suffixes -*y* and -*ful*

Read each sentence. Add the suffix -*y* or -*ful* to complete the underlined word.

1. The garden smells <u>flower</u> + _____.

2. Joel's smile showed he was <u>joy</u> + _____.

3. The <u>play</u> + _____ kitten

   knocked over a vase.

Circle the word that correctly completes each sentence.

4. I always look both ways before crossing the street.

   I am very _____.

   careful   **carefully**

5. The weather was bad today.

   It was very _____.

   rainful   **rainy**

6. My lemonade was _____ after
   the ice in it melted.

   watery   **waterful**

Proofread for Spelling

**Proofread Tony's letter. Circle six misspelled words.
Then write each misspelled word correctly.**

Dear Grandma and Grandpa,

    Last Friday, I got a new puppe. I was veray

surprised! Dad and Mom let me carey her home. She

was the onlee one I really liked. I'm going to name her

Peny. Don't you think that's a prettie name?

Love,
Tony

1. _____	4. _____
2. _____	5. _____
3. _____	6. _____

Spelling Words

Basic Words

1. happy
2. pretty
3. baby
4. very
5. puppy
6. funny
7. carry
8. lucky
9. only
10. sunny
11. penny
12. city

Write the Basic Word that answers each question.

7. I am very young. What am I? _____.

8. When I feel like this, I laugh. How do I feel? _____.

9. It is warm outside. How is the weather? _____.

10. Where do you see big buildings? _____.

Writing Quotations

✏️ **Underline the correct sentence.**

1. Dad said, "It snowed.".

Dad said "it snowed."

2. I asked, may I play outside?

I asked, "May I play outside?"

3. Mom said "have fun!"

Mom said, "Have fun!"

✏️ **Read each paragraph. Then write each paragraph correctly. Fix five mistakes in capitalization and punctuation.**

The cook said "i will make corn. He put corn in the bag.

Mama said "I will cook rice. She put rice in the bag.

_____

_____

_____

_____

Sentence Fluency

Sentences with Repeated Subjects	Sentences with Combined Subjects
The weather is rainy. The weather is cool.	The weather is rainy and cool.

Sentences with Repeated Subjects	Sentences with Combined Subjects
The students are reading. The students are learning.	The students are reading and learning.

Combine the sentences with repeating subjects.
Write the new sentence on the line.

1. The animals are eating. The animals are sleeping.

_____

2. They were running. They were playing.

_____

3. Sasha was reading. Sasha was writing.

_____

4. The country is growing. The country is changing.

_____

5. I am chatting. I am laughing.

_____

Words with *ar*

Circle the word that completes each sentence. Then write the word on the line.

1. Dee saw a bright _____ in the sky.

   state   **star**   **sat**

2. The dog in the yard started to _____.

   bark   **dark**   **bank**

3. The children played baseball at the _____.

   part   **paint**   **park**

4. Mom put milk in her shopping _____.

   charm   **chair**   **cart**

5. The cows go into the _____ at night.

   barn   **bean**   **brain**

6. Max is a _____ boy.

   smack   **smart**   **start**

Write two sentences. Use words spelled with *ar*.

7. _____

8. _____

Commas in Dates

The Signmaker's Assistant

Grammar: Commas in Dates and Places

A **date** tells the month, the number of the day, and the year. Use a **comma (,)** between the day and the year in a date.

The pet store opened on June 1, 2002.

Thinking Question
Which number shows the day, and which number shows the year?

Write the date in each sentence. Put a comma in the correct place.

1. Sally got her dog on February 12 2011.

_____

2. Josh's cat was born on April 30 2010.

_____

3. Mrs. Kane bought more fish food on January 1 2012.

_____

4. Mr. Kane went on vacation on July 12 2011.

_____

5. Carrie worked in the store until August 27 2012.

_____

Name _____ Date _____

Lesson 19
READER'S NOTEBOOK

The Signmaker's
Assistant
Phonics: Words with *ar*

Words with *ar*

Choose a word from the box to complete each sentence.
Write it on the line.

Word Bank

harm	shark	part	farm
artist	art	stars	park

1. Every Monday we have _____ class.

2. This is the _____ of the week

I like best.

3. I feel like a real _____ when I draw.

4. I painted a picture of trees in the _____.

5. Mark painted animals on a _____.

6. Darla painted many _____ in the

night sky.

Write two sentences. Use at least two words from the box.

7. _____

8. _____

Name _____ Date _____

Lesson 19
READER'S NOTEBOOK

The Signmaker's
Assistant
Spelling: Words with *ar*

Words with *ar*

Sort the Spelling Words by the number of letters in each word.

3 **4** **5**

1. _____   5. _____   12. _____

2. _____   6. _____   13. _____

3. _____   7. _____   14. _____

4. _____   8. _____

9. _____

10. _____

11. _____

Basic Words

1. car
2. dark
3. arm
4. star
5. park
6. yard
7. party
8. hard
9. farm
10. start
11. part
12. spark

Review Words

13. art
14. jar

Now, add to your lists. Add two *ar* words you know to each column.

15. _____   17. _____   19. _____

16. _____   18. _____   20. _____

Commas with Place Names

The Signmaker's Assistant

Grammar: Commas in Dates and Places

Use a **comma (,)** between the name of a city or town and the name of a state.

The gas station is in Dallas, Texas.

Thinking Question
Which word is the name of the city or town, and which word is the name of the state?

Write the city and state named in each sentence. Put a comma in the correct place.

1. The car breaks down after we leave Austin Texas.

_____

2. A truck tows the car to San Antonio Texas.

_____

3. A repairman calls a shop in Miami Florida.

_____

4. The shop sends car parts from Atlanta Georgia.

_____

5. Then we drive to Oakland California.

_____

Lesson 19
READER'S NOTEBOOK

The Signmaker's Assistant
Writing: Narrative Writing

Focus Trait: Organization
Beginning, Middle, End

Read the story below. Think about the beginning, middle, and end. Then write what each part tells you.

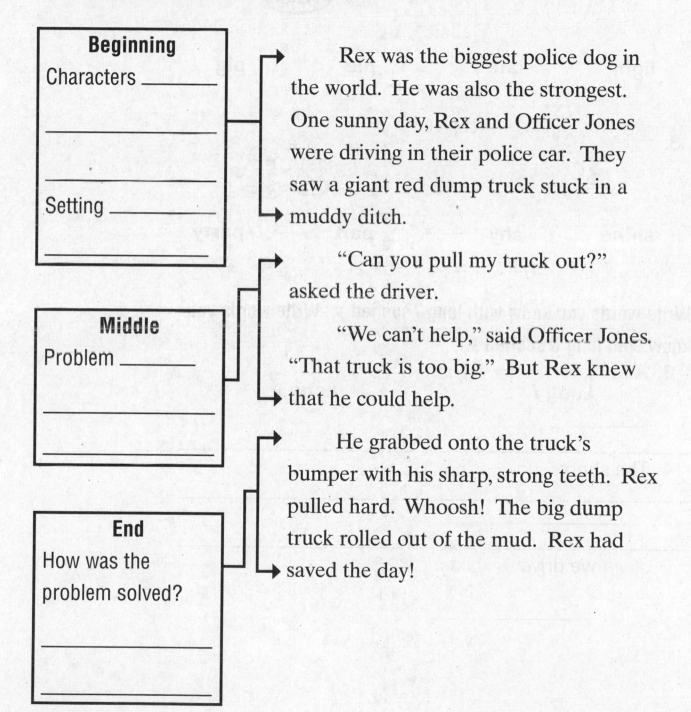

Beginning

Characters _____

_____

_____

Setting _____

_____

Rex was the biggest police dog in the world. He was also the strongest. One sunny day, Rex and Officer Jones were driving in their police car. They saw a giant red dump truck stuck in a muddy ditch.

"Can you pull my truck out?" asked the driver.

"We can't help," said Officer Jones. "That truck is too big." But Rex knew that he could help.

Middle

Problem _____

_____

_____

He grabbed onto the truck's bumper with his sharp, strong teeth. Rex pulled hard. Whoosh! The big dump truck rolled out of the mud. Rex had saved the day!

End

How was the problem solved?

_____

_____

Cumulative Review

**Circle the word that goes with each picture. Underline
the letters that spell the long *i* or long *e* sound.**

1.

    light   **late**

2.

    pie   **pig**

3.

    shine   **shy**

4.

    part   **party**

**Write words you know with long *i* spelled *y*. Write words you
know with long *e* spelled *y*.**

Long *i*	**Long *e***
_____	_____
_____	_____
_____	_____

Reader's Guide

The Signmaker's Assistant

Make a Sign

Hi. I'm Norman. I made a big mistake in this story.
I also learned some lessons. Look for the lessons
I learned.

Read page 128. Why was the signmaker important to the town?

_____

_____

Read page 129. What made people follow the directions on the signmaker's signs?

_____

_____

Read page 141. Why were the signs important?

_____

_____

Read page 149. What did the signmaker say after I apologized?

_____

_____

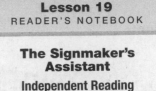

Now the sign shop is mine, and I need an assistant. Think about the work I did when I was the assistant. Use details and pictures from the story to see what a good signmaker assistant does.

Help Wanted

Signmaker's Assistant

The assistant will do these things:

1. _____

2. _____

3. _____

4. _____

5. _____

If you are interested, contact Norman at the Sign Shop.

Words with *ar*

Write the Spelling Word that goes with each picture.

1. _____

2. _____

3. _____

4. _____

5. _____

6. _____

Write the Spelling Word that matches each clue.

7. To begin _____

8. Where pigs and
   cows live _____

9. Not bright _____

10. The opposite of soft _____

11. Where grass grows _____

12. Not whole _____

13. A flash of light _____

14. A painting _____

Spelling Words

Basic Words
1. car
2. dark
3. arm
4. star
5. park
6. yard
7. party
8. hard
9. farm
10. start
11. part
12. spark

Review Words
13. art
14. jar

Name _____ Date _____

Commas in Parts of Letters

✏️ **Read this letter. It needs five commas. Write each comma where it belongs in this letter.**

Dear Jia

On May 2 2012, I visited Miami Florida. We had fun. I think you will like Tampa Florida, too.

Your friend

Ben

✏️ **Write the city and state named in each sentence. Put a comma in the correct place.**

1. The flower shop is in Portland Maine.

_____

2. Mrs. Longman calls from Los Angeles California.

_____

3. Frank Richards visits Seattle Washington.

_____

Name _____ Date _____

Lesson 19
READER'S NOTEBOOK

The Signmaker's Assistant
Vocabulary Strategies:
Shades of Meaning

Shades of Meaning

Choose the best word from the Word Bank to complete each sentence. Use every word.

```
Word Bank

tumble        slide        slip
```

1. The wall of mud began to _____ slowly down the hill.

2. Be careful not to _____ on the slimy seaweed!

3. Turning over and over, the child began to

   _____ down the grassy hill.

```
Word Bank

cool        cold        frozen
```

4. A _____ breeze is welcome after the day's heat.

5. You should wear a hat on a _____ and snowy day.

6. When the pond is _____, we can skate on it.

Proofread for Spelling

Proofread the invitation. Circle the six misspelled words.
Then write the correct spellings on the lines below.

Dear Kara,

You are invited to my paurty.
It will be in the parke on Center
Street. It is not heard to find.
We will starrt from my house
at 12:00. My mother will
drive us in her kar. We
will be home before dirk.

Your friend,
Angie

Spelling Words
Basic Words
1. car
2. dark
3. arm
4. star
5. park
6. yard
7. party
8. hard
9. farm
10. start
11. part
12. spark

1. _____   4. _____

2. _____   5. _____

3. _____   6. _____

Write these other Spelling Words in ABC order: *part, star,*
yard, farm, arm, spark.

7. _____   10. _____

8. _____   11. _____

9. _____   12. _____

Name _____ Date _____

Lesson 19
READER'S NOTEBOOK

The Signmaker's
Assistant
Grammar: Spiral Review

Writing Proper Nouns

✏️ **Write the name of each underlined word correctly.**

1. The store is closed on <u>thursday</u>.

_____

2. That day is <u>thanksgiving</u>.

_____

3. They put up a sign early in <u>november</u>.

_____

✏️ **Read the paragraphs. Write words from the box to tell when.**

My mom loves _____.

The holiday is _____. She wants

flowers. Dad buys them at Lou's Flower Shop.

Mom's birthday is in _____.

Dad loves _____. He wants

to sleep late. Mom says he gets to sleep late

_____!

Word Box

July
every Saturday
next Sunday
Mother's Day
Father's Day

Conventions

Not Correct	Correct
The sports shop opened on May 8 1998.	The sports shop opened on <u>May 8</u>, <u>1998</u>.

Not Correct	Correct
The soccer ball was made in Detroit Michigan.	The soccer ball was made in <u>Detroit</u>, <u>Michigan</u>.

Proofread the sentences for missing commas. Rewrite each sentence correctly.

1. The sports store opened on March 15 2005.

_____

2. It is in Charleston South Carolina.

_____

3. Mr. Thomas sold ice skates on December 1 2006.

_____

4. He sold beach balls on June 5 2007.

_____

5. He sold shells from Daytona Beach Florida.

_____

Words with *or*, *ore*

Write words to complete the sentences. Use words from the box.

porch	adore
story	Sport
more	before

1. This is a _____ about my dog.

2. His name is _____.

3. He sleeps on the _____.

4. We play _____ I go to school.

5. After school, we play some _____.

6. I _____ my dog!

Commas in a Series of Nouns

- A **series of nouns** is three or more nouns that appear together in a sentence.
- Use a comma after each noun in the series except for the last noun.

Sparky, Spike, Rover, and Leo are dogs.

Thinking Question
Are there three or more nouns being listed in a series?

Find the correct sentences. Circle the commas in each correct sentence.

1. Mom Dad, and Kim care for the dogs.

   Mom, Dad, and Kim care for the dogs.

   Mom, Dad, and, Kim, care for the dogs.

2. Dogs, cats, and birds are great pets.

   Dogs cats and birds are great pets.

   Dogs, cats, and, birds are great pets.

3. Max, Harry, and, Grace are puppies.

   Max, Harry, and Grace are puppies.

   Max, Harry, and Grace, are puppies.

4. Puppies need food, water, and, love.

   Puppies need food water and, love.

   Puppies need food, water, and love.

Words with *or, ore*

Write a word from the box to answer each riddle.

Word Bank

wore
short
chore
corn
snore
stork

1. a sound made when sleeping _____

2. a farm plant _____

3. a kind of bird _____

4. not tall _____

5. put on a coat _____

6. a small job _____

Write two sentences. Use two words from the box.

7. _____

8. _____

Name _____ Date _____

Words with *or, ore*

Sort the Basic Words.

Spelling Words

Basic Words
1. horn
2. story
3. fork
4. score
5. store
6. corn
7. morning
8. shore
9. short
10. born
11. tore
12. forget

Review Words
13. for
14. more

or Words	*ore* Words
1. _____	9. _____
2. _____	10. _____
3. _____	11. _____
4. _____	12. _____
5. _____	
6. _____	
7. _____	
8. _____	

Write one more *or* word you know. Then write one more *ore* word.

or Word	*ore* Word
13. _____	14. _____

Commas in a Series of Verbs

- A **series of verbs** is three or more verbs that appear together in a sentence.
- Use a comma after each verb in a series except the last verb.

Hamster runs, leaps, and waves.

Thinking Question
Are there three or more verbs listed in a series?

Look at the underlined verbs in each sentence. Write each sentence correctly. Put commas in the correct places.

1. Chipmunk <u>slips falls and cries.</u>

_____

2. Hamster <u>dashes jumps and helps.</u>

_____

3. Chipmunk <u>smiles skips and dances.</u>

_____

4. The animals <u>wave cheer and shout.</u>

_____

5. Hamster <u>laughs bows and leaves.</u>

_____

Lesson 20
READER'S NOTEBOOK

Focus Trait: Organization
Interesting Beginnings

Dex: The Heart of a Hero
Writing: Narrative Writing

Uninteresting Beginning	Interesting Beginning
Once there was a cat named Freddy.	Freddy was a fluffy black cat. He was so smart that he solved mysteries for his friends.

Write two different beginnings for a story about a deep-sea diving dog. Make each beginning interesting. Check the one you like better.

1. _____

_____

_____

_____

2. _____

_____

_____

_____

Cumulative Review

Read the clue. Circle the word that matches.

1. A dog will do this.   store   **bark**   shark

2. It means **begin**.   **start**   dart   north

3. It is part of the body.   farm   more   **arm**

4. You play here.   star   **park**   pork

5. It means **big**.   **large**   porch   spark

6. You ride in this.   art   **car**   born

Name _____   Date _____

Lesson 20
READER'S NOTEBOOK

**Dex: The Heart
of a Hero**
Independent Reading

Reader's Guide

Dex: The Heart of a Hero

Write a Newspaper Article

The newspaper wants to write an article about
the new superhero in town. Use details and
illustrations from the text to find information for the
article about Dex.

Read pages 171–173. How did Dex prepare for being a superhero?

_____

_____

Read pages 174–175. How did Dex know he was ready to be a superhero?

_____

_____

Read pages 178–179. What were some ways Dex helped?

_____

_____

_____

Read pages 184–185. How did Dex get Cleevis as a partner?

_____

_____

_____

Name _____ Date _____

Lesson 20
READER'S NOTEBOOK

Dex: The Heart
of a Hero
Independent Reading

Write a newspaper article about Dex. Tell
what Dex does to show he is a hero. Include
an illustration with a caption.

❧ New Superhero in Town! ❧

What Dex Does	Dex's Advice on Becoming a Superhero
_____	_____
_____	_____
_____	_____
_____	_____
_____	_____
	_____
	_____
	_____
	_____
	_____
_____	_____

Words with *or*, *ore*

Write a Basic Word for each meaning.

1. A place where you buy things _____

2. The opposite of *tall* _____

3. Early hours of the day _____

4. A food _____

5. Something you blow _____

6. Land near water _____

Complete each sentence with a Basic Word.

7. Do not _____ your homework!

8. I was _____ on the 4th of July.

9. Please read me a _____.

10. I always use a _____ to eat.

11. Alan _____ his jacket when

 he fell.

12. We won by a _____

 of 3 to 2.

Spelling Words
Basic Words
1. horn
2. story
3. fork
4. score
5. store
6. corn
7. morning
8. shore
9. short
10. born
11. tore
12. forget
Review Words
13. for
14. more

RAMS © EAGLES

Commas in a Series

✎ **Draw a line under each correct sentence.**

1. Super Cat visits the park, school, and, playground.

Super Cat visits the park, school, and playground.

Super Cat, visits the, park, school and playground.

2. She saves a butterfly, worm, and ladybug.

She saves a, butterfly, worm, and ladybug.

She saves a butterfly, worm and ladybug.

3. Mama Papa, and Baby Cat, are happy!

Mama, Papa and Baby, Cat are happy!

Mama, Papa, and Baby Cat are happy!

✎ **Write each sentence. Use commas correctly.**

4. The penguins waddle jump and slide.

_____

5. They dive splash and swim.

_____

6. People watch point and smile.

_____

Name _____ Date _____

Lesson 20
READER'S NOTEBOOK

Dex: The Heart of a Hero
Vocabulary Strategies:
Prefix *over-*

Prefix *over-*

Read each sentence. Fill in the blank with one of the words in the box.

> **Word Box**
>
> overlooked   overcrowded   overboard
> overeat   overdue   overflowed

1. I don't want to _____ at

dinner. I want to save room for dessert!

2. Too many people came to the party, so the room

was _____.

3. Tom can't find his book on the shelf. Maybe he

_____ it.

4. I poured too much milk in my cup, and it

_____.

5. The movies we rented are _____.

We should have returned them last week.

6. I went on a boat ride last week, and my sunglasses

fell _____!

Name _____ Date _____

Proofread for Spelling

Proofread the ad. Cross out the five misspelled words.
Then write the correct spellings in the margin.

Come to our grocery stour!

Big sale on korn!

The sale begins at 8:00 in the mourning.

Sale items are in shart supply.

They won't last long!

Don't furget!

Unscramble the letters to spell a Basic Word.
Write the word on the line.

Spelling Words
Basic Words
1. horn
2. story
3. fork
4. score
5. store
6. corn
7. morning
8. shore
9. short
10. born
11. tore
12. forget

1. rnbo _____

2. orkf _____

3. soreh _____

4. hnor _____

5. erot _____

6. styor _____

7. crose _____

Writing Book Titles

Rewrite each sentence. Write the book titles correctly.
Remember to use capital letters when needed.

1. My favorite book is the cat in the hat.

_____

2. Did Dr. Rames write the book taking care of pets?

_____

Fix the mistakes in the paragraph. Write the
paragraph correctly.

Mr. Grady owns a book store. Today, Lynn buys
the book caring for dogs. Mr. Grady also sells her
another book. This one is called how to keep a bird.

_____

_____

_____

Sentence Fluency

Short, Choppy Sentences	Smoother Sentence with Commas
Sam read the story. Izzy read the story. Mario read the story.	Sam, Izzy, and Mario read the story.

Short, Choppy Sentences	Smoother Sentence with Commas
The monkeys had bananas. The monkeys had apples. The monkeys had carrots.	The monkeys had bananas, apples, and carrots.

Read each group of sentences. Combine the three sentences. Use commas correctly.

1. The monkeys climbed trees.

The monkeys climbed vines.

The monkeys climbed ropes.

_____

2. Owl watched the monkeys.

Ant watched the monkeys.

Tiger watched the monkeys.

_____

3. The monkeys jumped on the rocks.

The monkeys climbed on the rocks.

The monkeys ate on the rocks.

_____

Name _____ Date _____

Unit 4
READER'S NOTEBOOK

Where Do Polar Bears Live?
Segment 1
Independent Reading

Reader's Guide

Where Do Polar Bears Live?

Polar Bear Research Log

Read pages 8–19. Imagine you are a scientist who studies polar bears. Complete the pages of your research log. Take notes and make sketches.

Age: Newborn

What does it look like?

_____

_____

_____

_____

_____

_____

_____

What does it do?

_____

_____

_____

Name _____ Date _____

Unit 4
READER'S NOTEBOOK

Where Do
Polar Bears Live?
Segment 1
Independent Reading

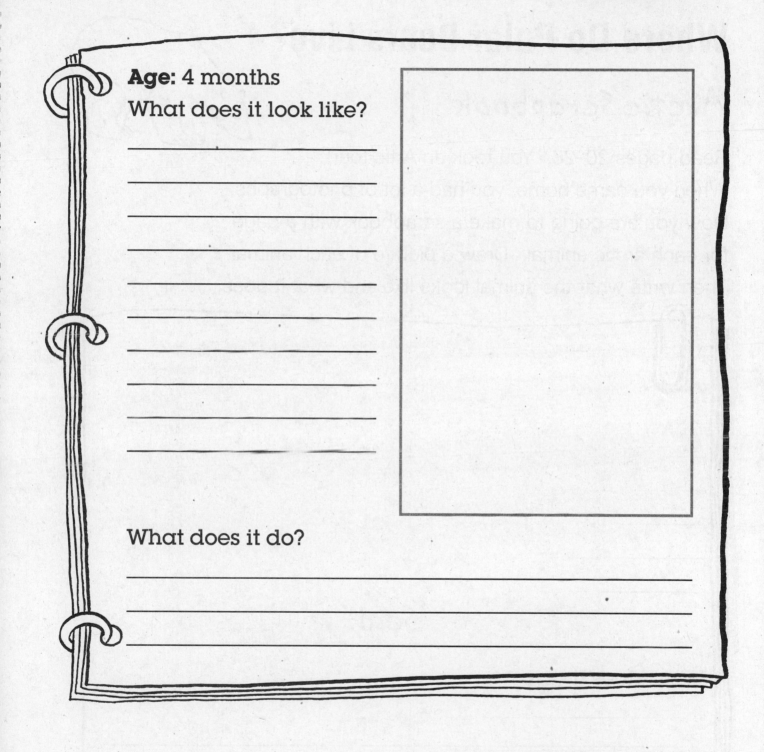

Age: 4 months

What does it look like?

_____

_____

_____

_____

_____

_____

_____

_____

What does it do?

_____

_____

_____

Name _____ Date _____

Unit 4
READER'S NOTEBOOK

Where Do
Polar Bears Live?
Segment 2
Independent Reading

Reader's Guide

Where Do Polar Bears Live?

Arctic Scrapbook

Read pages 20–28. You took an Artic tour!
When you came home, you had a lot of photographs.
Now you are going to make a scrapbook with a page
for each arctic animal. Draw a picture of each animal.
Then write what the animal looks like and what it does.

Seal

_____

_____

_____

Name _____ Date _____

Unit 4
READER'S NOTEBOOK

**Where Do
Polar Bears Live?**
Segment 2
Independent Reading

Arctic Fox

Today we saw an arctic fox.

_____

_____

_____

Name _____ Date _____

Unit 4
READER'S NOTEBOOK
**Where Do
Polar Bears Live?**
Segment 3
Independent Reading

Where Do Polar Bears Live?

Help Save the Polar Bears!

Read pages 29–35. Each year, the Arctic ice melts and freezes. However, less ice freezes every year. Write reasons why this is a problem for polar bears.

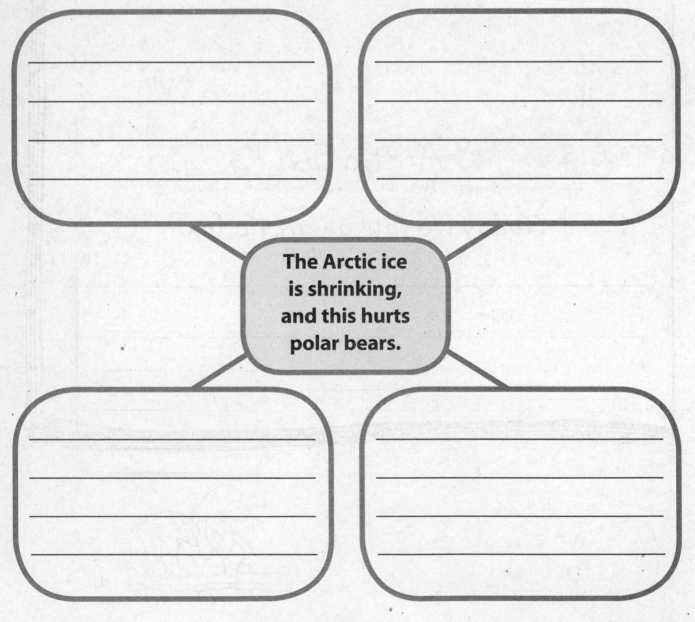

The Arctic ice is shrinking, and this hurts polar bears.

Name _____ Date _____

Unit 4
READER'S NOTEBOOK

**Where Do
Polar Bears Live?**
Segment 3
Independent Reading

The author provides interesting facts about polar bears. Use pages 29–35 to create an animal fact card about polar bears. Draw a picture and write facts.

Polar Bears

Did you know?

- _____
  _____

- _____
  _____

- _____
  _____

- _____
  _____

Words with *er*

Circle the word that fits in each sentence.

Underline the letters that stand for the *er* sound.

Then write the word to complete the sentence.

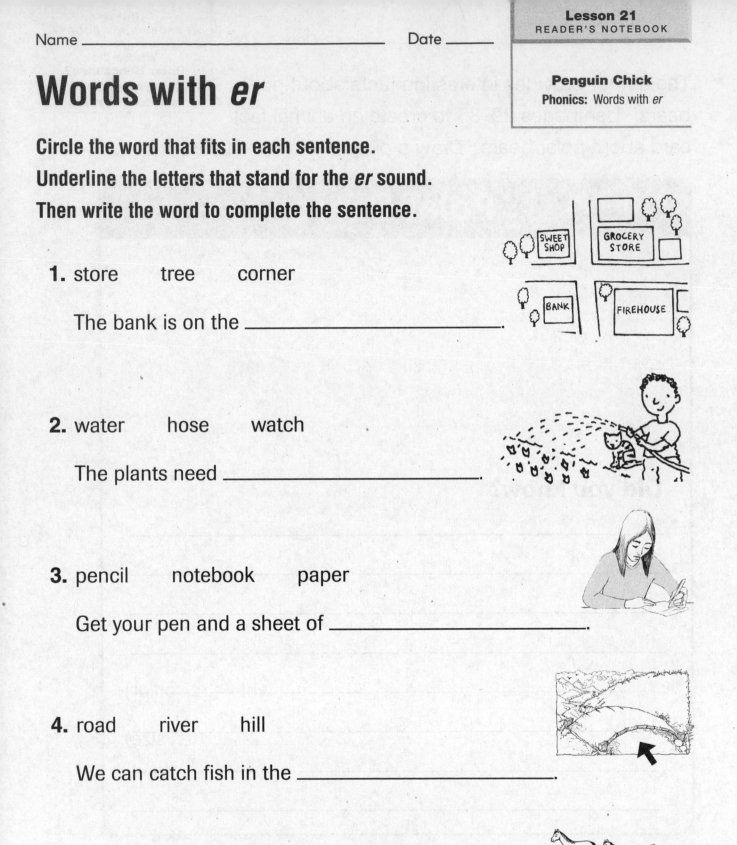

1. store   tree   corner

The bank is on the _____.

2. water   hose   watch

The plants need _____.

3. pencil   notebook   paper

Get your pen and a sheet of _____.

4. road   river   hill

We can catch fish in the _____.

5. head   herd   horses

A group of horses is called a _____.

How Things Look

An **adjective** is a word that tells how something looks.

Adjectives can tell size, color, shape, or how many.

Penguins look short.

Thinking Question
Which word tells more about how something looks?

Write the adjective from the box that best fits each sentence. Use the clues in ( ).

round	small	four	black

1. I see _____ penguins on the ice.
   (tell how many)

2. The penguins stand in a _____ circle.
   (tell shape)

3. They are _____ and white. (tell color)

4. The baby penguin is _____. (tell size)

Words with *er*

Put the letters together to write a word with *er*.

1. f + a + t + h + er = _____

2. c + o + m + p + u + t + er = _____

3. w + h + i + s + k + er + s = _____

4. t + o + a + s + t + er = _____

5. b + a + k + er = _____

Now use the *er* words you wrote to complete the sentences below.

6. I put my bread in the _____.

7. My cat has long _____ on her face.

8. The _____ sells cookies and pies.

9. I eat dinner with my mother and _____.

10. I play games on the _____.

Words with *er*

Sort the Spelling Words.

**Basic
Words**
1. father
2. over
3. under
4. herd
5. water
6. verb
7. paper
8. cracker
9. offer
10. cover
11. germ
12. master

**Review
Words**
13. fern
14. ever

Words that end in *er*

1. _____

2. _____

3. _____

4. _____

5. _____

6. _____

7. _____

8. _____

9. _____

10. _____

Words with *er* in middle

11. _____

12. _____

13. _____

14. _____

**Underline the letter or letters that make the *er* sound in
each word.**

How Things Taste and Smell

Adjectives can tell how something tastes.

Adjectives can also tell how something smells.

The ocean smells fishy.

The water tastes salty.

Thinking Question
Which word tells more about how something tastes or smells?

Find the adjective in each sentence. The adjective tells more about the underlined word. Write the adjective.

1. The penguins eat the tasty <u>fish</u>.

_____

2. They drink the salty <u>water</u>.

_____

3. The penguins like smelly <u>seafood</u>.

_____

4. They smell the fresh <u>air</u>.

_____

5. They love the taste of sweet <u>squid</u>.

_____

Focus Trait: Word Choice Using Exact Words

Without Exact Words	With Exact Words
In Antarctica there is <u>nothing</u> to build a nest with.	In Antarctica there are **no twigs**, **leaves**, **grass, or mud** to build a nest with.

A. Read each sentence. Replace each underlined word with more exact words.

Without Exact Words	With Exact Words
1. The egg stays <u>comfortable</u> in the brood patch.	The egg stays _____ in the brood patch.
2. The penguin fathers <u>are</u> together in a group.	The penguin fathers _____ together in a group.

B. Pair/Share Work with a partner to brainstorm exact words to replace the underlined words in the sentence.

Without Exact Words	With Exact Words
3. With his <u>mouth</u>, the penguin father <u>puts</u> the egg onto his <u>feet</u>.	
4. After the chick <u>comes out of the egg</u>, its wet feathers <u>change</u>.	

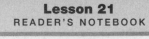

Words with *ir, ur*

1. Write **X** on the bigger **bird**.

Write **bird**.

_____

2. Draw stripes on the **shirt**.

Write **shirt**.

_____

3. Color the one we can **burn** to

make light. Write **burn**.

_____

4. Circle the **birthday** cake.

Write **birthday**.

_____

5. Write **X** on **Thursday**.

Write **Thursday**.

Monday	Tuesday	Wednesday	Thursday	Friday
		1	2	3

_____

Reader's Guide

Penguin Chick

Make a Scrapbook

Make a scrapbook for the baby penguin. Draw and write about what happens as the chick grows.

Read pages 214–217. Draw and write about what happened today.

_____
_____
_____
_____

Read page 218. Draw and write about what happened today.

_____
_____
_____
_____

Read page 220. Draw and write about what happened today.

_____
_____
_____
_____

Read page 222. Draw and write about what happened today.

_____
_____
_____
_____

Read page 224. Draw and write about what happened today.

_____
_____
_____
_____

Words with *er*

Write the Spelling Word that means almost the same as each word.

1. blanket _____

2. above _____

3. share _____

4. below _____

5. group _____

6. dad _____

Write the Spelling Word that rhymes with each word.

7. worm _____

8. turn _____

9. daughter _____

10. curb _____

11. clever _____

12. plaster _____

Spelling Words

Basic Words
1. father
2. over
3. under
4. herd
5. water
6. verb
7. paper
8. cracker
9. offer
10. cover
11. germ
12. master

Review Words
13. fern
14. ever

How Things Feel and Sound

Write the adjective from the box that best fits each
sentence. Use the clues in ( ).

howling	icy	loud	slippery

1. Penguins stand in the _____ wind. (sound)

2. The father penguin has a _____ voice. (sound)

3. Penguins swim in _____ oceans. (feel)

4. They catch _____ fish with their beaks. (feel)

Find the adjective in each sentence. Write the word that tells more
about the underlined word.

5. The penguins hear splashing <u>water</u>.

_____

6. They step on the pointy <u>rocks</u>.

_____

7. Penguin chicks have fluffy <u>feathers</u>.

_____

8. The penguins make whistling <u>sounds</u>.

_____

Name _____ Date _____

Lesson 21
READER'S NOTEBOOK

Penguin Chick
Vocabulary Strategies:
Dictionary Entry

Dictionary Entry

Read each sentence. Use the dictionary entries to help
you decide what the word means. Write the definition
on the line.

creature	**1.** an animal **2.** a strange or imaginary living thing
shuffle	**1.** to walk without picking up your feet **2.** to mix cards or papers so they are in a different order
swallow[1]	to make food or drink go down your throat
swallow[2]	a small bird with pointed wings and a tail with two points
webbed	**1.** having skin that connects the toes or fingers **2.** made of something that looks or feels like a web: *My purse has a webbed strap.*

1. Kim had to <u>swallow</u> her food before she could talk.

_____

2. I will <u>shuffle</u> the cards before we start the game.

_____

3. We saw a silly blue <u>creature</u> on TV.

_____

4. Frogs have <u>webbed</u> feet to help them swim and hop.

_____

Proofread for Spelling

Circle the misspelled words in the items below. Then write the correct spellings on the lines.

Make a Good Snack

1. Wash your hands with soap and wotter. You do not want to get a jerm on your snack.

_____   _____

2. Cuver a craker with peanut butter. Place another one on top.

_____   _____

3. Put a payper napkin undr your snack. Pour a glass of milk.

_____   _____

4. You are now the mayster of snacks! Why not ofer one to your mother or fathr?

_____   _____   _____

Unscramble the letters to spell a Basic Word.

5. berv _____   **7.** dher _____

6. ervo _____

Spelling Words
Basic Words
1. father
2. over
3. under
4. herd
5. water
6. verb
7. paper
8. cracker
9. offer
10. cover
11. germ
12. master

Reflexive Pronouns

✎ **Circle the correct pronoun to complete each sentence.**
Then write the sentence.

1. I bought (ourselves, myself) a book about the South Pole.

_____

2. My partner and I wrote a report by (ourselves, myself).

_____

3. We taught (ourselves, myself) a lot about penguins.

_____

4. I surprised (ourselves, myself) by how much I learned.

_____

5. The teacher said we should be very pleased with
(ourselves, myself).

_____

Sentence Fluency

Short, Choppy Sentences	Longer, Smooth Sentence
The penguins were hungry. The penguins were tired.	The penguins were hungry and tired.

Read each pair of sentences. Join the sentences using <u>and</u> between the two adjectives. Write the new sentence.

1. The penguin was cold.

   The penguin was wet.

   _____

2. The rain was heavy.

   The rain was pounding.

   _____

3. The egg was warm.

   The egg was covered.

   _____

4. The sky was cloudy.

   The sky was dark.

   _____

Homophones

Read the two homophones in each box. Then choose the word that goes on each line. Read the completed sentences.

1. I _____ my bike on

a bumpy _____ .

rode
road

2. Let's _____ at the

store to buy _____ .

meat
meet

3. Sam read a _____ about

a dog wagging its _____ .

tale
tail

4. I can _____ the waves of the

_____ crashing on the shore.

sea
see

5. Jason is _____ from

being sick all _____ .

weak
week

Adjectives

- An **adjective** is a word that tells more about another word.
- Numbers are special adjectives that tell how many.

Julian made <u>one</u> kite.

Gloria tied <u>two</u> wishes to her kite.

Thinking Question
Which word tells how many?

Draw a line under each adjective that tells how many.

Write the noun it tells about.

1. Gloria had two pigtails. _____

2. Julian tied five wishes to his kite. _____

3. Gloria and Julian walked six blocks. _____

4. Julian counted twelve rocks from his collection.

_____

5. They found one nest. _____

Name _____ Date _____

Lesson 22
READER'S·NOTEBOOK

**Gloria Who Might Be
My Best Friend**
Phonics: Homophones

Homophones

Choose a word from the box to complete each sentence.
Write the word on the line. Read each completed sentence.

Word Bank

be	blew	rode	weak	two
bee	main	road	sea	too
blue	mane	week	see	

1. The wind _____ the door open.

2. Please save _____ seats at lunch.

3. This flower has a _____ on it!

4. Tim _____ his dad's bike.

5. There are seven days in one _____.

6. I like to swim in the salty _____.

7. What is the _____ idea on that page?

8. There is _____ much noise.

9. My favorite color is _____.

10. It is too dark to _____.

Homophones

Write the Spelling Word that sounds the same as the given word.

1. sea _____

2. bee _____

3. week _____

4. two _____

5. meet _____

6. tail _____

7. mane _____

Spelling Words
Basic Words
1. meet
2. meat
3. week
4. weak
5. mane
6. main
7. tail
8. tale
9. be
10. bee
11. too
12. two
Review Words
13. sea
14. see

Now sort the Spelling Words by vowel sounds. The first one is done for you.

Long *e*	Long *a*	*oo* sound
sea _____	_____	_____
_____	_____	_____
_____	_____	
_____	_____	
_____		
_____		
_____		

Adjectives with -*er* and -*est*

- Add -<u>er</u> to adjectives to compare **two** people, animals, places, or things.
- Add -<u>est</u> to compare **more than two** people, animals, places, or things.

Jan is tall.

Beth is <u>taller</u> than Jan.

Nina is thc <u>tallest</u> friend of all.

Thinking Question
How many people, animals, places, or things are being compared?

Write the correct word for each sentence.

1. Beth is _____ than Nina.
   (quieter   quietest)

2. Jan is the _____ person of all.
   (quieter   quietest)

3. Nina has _____ hair than Jan.
   (shorter   shortest)

4. Jan has the _____ hair in the class.
   (longer   longest)

5. Jan has a _____ dog than Nina.
   (smaller   smallest)

Name _____ Date _____

Lesson 22
READER'S NOTEBOOK

Gloria Who Might Be
My Best Friend
Writing: Informative Writing

Focus Trait: Organization Details

A. Read each paragraph. Cross out the detail that does not support the main idea.

1. Gloria and Julian are different in some ways.

   They both know how to fly a kite.

   Gloria is a fast runner, but Julian runs slowly.

   Gloria can turn a cartwheel, but Julian can't.

2. Gloria and Julian are alike in some ways.

   Julian knows the best way to make wishes, and Gloria doesn't.

   They like playing outside.

   They go to the same school.

B. Read each main idea. Give a detail that supports the main idea.

Pair/Share Work with a partner to brainstorm possible details for each main idea.

Main Idea	Detail
3. Doctors and nurses are alike in many ways.	
4. Cats and dogs are alike in some ways.	

Base Words and Endings -er, -est

Follow the direction for each question.

1. Who is **oldest**? Circle her.

2. Circle the **biggest** fish.

3. Circle the animal with the **lightest** color fur.

4. Who is **younger**? Circle him.

5. Circle the **taller** animal.

Write the correct word in the sentence.

6. longer   longest   Anna's skirt is

_____ than Amy's skirt.

7. faster   fastest   That is the

_____ car I have ever seen.

8. thinner   thinnest   Eric is

_____ than his dad.

Name _____ Date _____

Lesson 22
READER'S NOTEBOOK

Gloria Who Might Be
My Best Friend
Independent Reading

Reader's Guide

Gloria Who Might Be
My Best Friend

Gloria Retells the Story

Now Gloria is going to tell the story of meeting Julian. What will she say? Use the text to help Gloria tell and illustrate the story.

Read pages 248–249. How would Gloria tell this part of the story?

_____

_____

_____

Read pages 250–251. How would Gloria tell this part of the story?

_____

_____

_____

Read pages 254–255. Think about what Gloria might wish for. Draw and write about her two wishes.

_____

_____

_____

Read pages 257–261. How would Gloria tell this part of the story?

_____

_____

_____

Homophones

**Circle the correct Spelling Word to complete each sentence.
Write the Spelling Word on the line.**

1. A horse has a (mane, main). _____

2. Our town has one (mane, main) street. _____

3. I like to eat (meat, meet). _____

4. It is fun to (meat, meet) a new friend. _____

5. Seven days make a (week, weak). _____

6. A (week, weak) person is not strong. _____

7. I read a (tail, tale) about a cat with a long (tail, tale).

_____   _____

8. Who will (bee, be) afraid of a (bee, be)?

_____   _____

9. You can (sea, see) the (sea, see) at the beach.

_____   _____

10. (Too, Two) hippos are (too, two) big for the pond.

_____   _____

Spelling Words

Basic Words
1. meet
2. meat
3. week
4. weak
5. mane
6. main
7. tail
8. tale
9. be
10. bee
11. too
12. two

Review Words
13. sea
14. see

Using Adjectives

Draw a line under the word in ( ) that correctly completes each sentence.

1. Luis is (a, an) pal.

2. He goes on (a, an) airplane to visit George.

3. George cleans (a, an) attic upstairs.

4. Luis stays for (a, an) week.

5. The boys play in (an, the) park.

Write the correct word for each sentence.

6. The pond is _____ than the pool.
(deeper   deepest)

7. Luis is the _____ swimmer of all.
(faster   fastest)

8. Monday was _____ than Sunday.
(warmer   warmest)

9. January was the _____ month of the year.
(colder   coldest)

10. George is _____ than Luis.
(older   oldest)

Name _____ Date _____

Lesson 22
READER'S NOTEBOOK

Gloria Who Might Be
My Best Friend
Vocabulary Strategies: Idioms

Idioms

Read each sentence. Choose the meaning from the box that could replace the underlined words. Write the meaning on the line.

Meanings

stay cheerful   very special to him   understands what to do
does her best   tight and uncomfortable

1. Kim's grandpa is proud of her. She is <u>the apple of his eye.</u>

   _____

2. Sally has been at her job for a long time, so she <u>knows the ropes.</u>

   _____

3. Jen had a good day at school. She always <u>puts her best foot forward.</u>

   _____

4. Jay is sad, so Mel told him to <u>keep his chin up.</u>

   _____

5. I am so nervous! My stomach is <u>tied in knots.</u>

   _____

Proofread for Spelling

Proofread the letter. Circle the misspelled words. Then write the correct spellings on the lines below.

Dear Jen,

    We moved into our new house. It is on Mane Street. We have too trees in the yard. I wanted to climb one, but Mom said it was two week.

    Lucky likes our new yard. He runs around and wags his tale. That silly dog bit at a be. I wonder if he thought it was meet to eat.

    This weak I start my new school. I hope I'll meat someone who wants to bee friends. I know we will have story time, and I think my new teacher is going to read a tail every day. Remember the story about the lion that lost his main?

    I miss you a lot. I hope you can come see me soon.

               Your Friend,

               Max

Spelling Words

Basic Words
1. meet
2. meat
3. week
4. weak
5. mane
6. main
7. tail
8. tale
9. be
10. bee
11. too
12. two

Review Words
13. sea
14. see

1. _____ 7. _____
2. _____ 8. _____
3. _____ 9. _____
4. _____ 10. _____
5. _____ 11. _____
6. _____ 12. _____

Subject-Verb Agreement

✎ **Circle the correct verb to go with each subject.**

1. She (play, plays) with me.

2. He (wish, wishes) for good luck.

3. We (throw, throws) a penny in the fountain.

4. They (hope, hopes) her wish comes true.

✎ **Proofread the paragraph. Circle the four verbs with the wrong endings. Then write each sentence correctly on the lines below.**

Julia is my best friend. She laugh at my jokes.

We watches baseball games. She give me sandwiches.

We shares our toys, too.

1. _____

2. _____

3. _____

4. _____

Name _____ Date _____

Lesson 22
READER'S NOTEBOOK

**Gloria Who Might Be
My Best Friend**
Grammar: Connect to Writing

Ideas

My friend has a new dog.

His dog is <u>smaller</u> than my dog.

His dog is the <u>smallest</u> of all the dogs.

Rewrite the paragraph. Replace each underlined adjective with words from the box that compare.

the fastest of all	longer than my arm
stronger today than yesterday	the highest of all the kites

My friend Bob makes a kite. The tail is <u>long</u>. His

kite looks like a bird. Bob takes the bird kite to the

park. The wind is <u>strong</u>. Many people are flying their

kites. The bird kite is <u>fast</u>. It flies <u>high</u>.

_____

_____

_____

_____

_____

_____

Suffixes *-y, -ly, -ful*

Circle the word that matches each picture. Write the word and underline the suffix.

1.

wonder   windy   _____

2.

helpful   hopping   _____

3.

snoring   snowy   _____

4.

safely   softer   _____

5.

careful   hurting   _____

The Goat in the Rug
Grammar: Irregular Verbs

Have, Has, and Had

- *Have*, *has*, and *had* are **irregular verbs**.
- Use *have* and *has* to tell about present time.
- Use *had* to tell about something that happened in the past.

Subject	Present	Past
We	have	had
Glenda	has	had
He, She, It	has	had
Ken and Marti	have	had
They	have	had

Jean **has** a new rug now.

Dee and Ben **have** a red rug now.

We **had** a blue rug years ago.

Thinking Question
When does the action take place and who is doing it?

Circle the word that correctly completes each sentence.

1. Carrie (have, has) two rugs.

2. Last week she (had, have) three rugs.

3. Now Gus and Lee (had, have) her old rug.

4. Carrie (had, have) no room for her rug.

5. Gus and Lee (has, had) room.

6. They (has, have) a big attic.

Grade 2, Unit 5

Suffixes *-y, -ly, -ful*

Choose a word from the box to complete each sentence.
Then read each sentence aloud with a partner.

> **Word Bank**
>
> | **-y** | **-ly** | **-ful** |
> |---|---|---|
> | rusty | quickly | careful |
> | windy | sadly | helpful |
> | | safely | painful |

1. Be _____ when you
cross the street.

2. _____ put the leash on Rover.

3. The old metal gate is all _____.

4. The boy looked _____ at
his broken toy.

5. The splinter in my finger was _____.

6. Put the money _____ in
your pocket.

7. Thank you for being so _____.

8. It's so _____ that my hat
blew away.

Suffixes *-ly*, *-ful*

Sort the Basic Words by the suffixes *-ly* and *-ful*.

Spelling Words

-ly

-ful

Word + *ly*

1. _____
2. _____
3. _____
4. _____
5. _____

Word + *ful*

6. _____
7. _____
8. _____
9. _____
10. _____
11. _____
12. _____

Basic Words

1. helpful
2. sadly
3. hopeful
4. thankful
5. slowly
6. wishful
7. kindly
8. useful
9. safely
10. painful
11. mouthful
12. weakly

Underline the suffix in each Basic Word.

Do, Does, and Did

- *Do*, *does*, and *did* are **irregular verbs**.
- Use *do* and *does* to tell about present time.
- Use *did* to tell about something that happened in the past.

Subject	Present	Past
We	do	did
Janet	does	did
He, She, It	does	did
Pedro and Sam	do	did
They	do	did

They **did** their best work with Jake.

He **does** square patterns.

We **do** striped patterns together.

Thinking Question
When does the action take place and who is doing it?

✏️ **Circle the correct word for each sentence.**

1. Last week they (do, did) some patterns with Jake.

2. Jake (do, does) great patterns.

3. Yesterday, he (do, did) squares and triangles.

4. Now we (do, does) circles together.

5. He (do, does) his own pattern.

Focus Trait: Word Choice
Synonyms

Writer's Words	Students' Own Words with Synonyms
You can <u>make</u> wool <u>beautiful</u> colors by <u>soaking</u> it in <u>dye</u>.	You can <u>turn</u> wool <u>pretty</u> colors by <u>dipping</u> it in <u>coloring</u>.

Read the words a writer wrote. Then rewrite the sentence in your own words, using synonyms.

Writer's Words	Your Own Words with Synonyms
1. You can <u>spin</u> wool into <u>threads</u> of yarn.	You can _____ wool into _____ of yarn.
2. A loom can be <u>built</u> using four <u>poles</u>.	A loom can be _____ using four _____.
3. You <u>start</u> weaving at the <u>bottom</u> of the loom.	You _____ weaving at the _____ of the loom.

Syllables *-tion, -ture*

Read the two words in each item below. Think about how the two words are alike. Then write the missing *-tion* or *-ture* word from the Word Bank that fits with each pair of words.

Word Bank

-tion	**-ture**
lotion	creature
vacation	picture
fraction	capture
nation	nature

1. trip, travel, _____

2. animal, beast, _____

3. piece, part of, _____

4. grab, catch, _____

5. a drawing, a painting, a _____

6. weather, plants, _____

7. city, state, _____

8. sunblock, hand cream, _____

Reader's Guide

The Goat in the Rug

Draw and Label a Picture

This story tells how a Navajo woman uses her goat's wool to weave a beautiful rug. Read and answer the questions about the story.

Read pages 281–282. What does Glenmae do first?

_____

Read page 284. What does Glenmae do in this part of the story?

_____

Read page 285. What does Glenmae do with Geraldine's wool now?

_____

Read pages 286–289. What else does Glenmae do?

_____

Read pages 292–294. What does Glenmae do last?

_____

Name _____ Date _____

In this story, Glenmae uses many tools. Find four tools in the story. Write and draw them in the order they are used. Write a sentence telling what Glenmae does with each tool.

The tool Glenmae uses first is the _____
She uses the scissors to _____
_____

The tool Glenmae uses second is the _____
She uses the tub to _____
_____

The tool Glenmae uses third is the _____
She uses the comb to _____
_____

The tool Glenmae uses fourth is the _____
She uses the spindle to _____
_____

Suffixes *-ly, -ful*

Write the Spelling Word that matches each meaning.

Spelling Words
Basic Words
1. helpful
2. sadly
3. hopeful
4. thankful
5. slowly
6. wishful
7. kindly
8. useful
9. safely
10. painful
11. mouthful
12. weakly

1. In a slow way _____

2. Wishing for something _____

3. In a way with no energy _____

4. Having hope _____

5. In a sad way _____

6. Giving help _____

7. Being kind _____

8. Being put to use _____

9. In a way that won't hurt you _____

10. A lot of food in your mouth _____

11. Full of thanks _____

12. Full of pain _____

Irregular Verbs

Circle the verb that correctly completes each sentence.

1. Last week the goat and lamb (have, had) long hair.

2. Yesterday they (have, had) a hair cut.

3. The lamb (has, have) short hair now.

4. The goat (has, have) short hair, too.

5. Now we (have, had) wool to make a rug.

Write the correct verb to finish each sentence.

6. Gerry _____ something fun.
   (do   does)

7. Tonya and Raj _____ a dance on the rug.
   (do   does)

8. They _____ their favorite dance yesterday.
   (do   did)

9. Gerry _____ his best when he jumped.
   (did   do)

10. He _____ his best right now.
   (do   does)

Compound Words

Name _____ Date _____

Draw a line between the words that make up each compound word in the Word Bank. Use what you know about the shorter words to predict the compound word's meaning. Complete each sentence by writing the compound word whose meaning fits the best.

Word Bank

doormat   rosebush   backyard   doorbell
mailbox   sandbox   sidewalk   trashcan

1. The children sat in the _____ and

   filled the pails with sand.

2. "Let's go to the _____ ," said Robert.

   "I want to climb the oak tree."

3. Mr. Hendricks wiped his feet on the _____

   before going into the house.

4. We thought we heard the _____ ring,

   but nobody was there.

5. Larry found two letters in his _____ .

6. The _____ is full. I better empty it.

7. "Ouch," said Theresa. "This _____

   has a lot of thorns.

8. Sometimes Steve skateboards on the _____.

Proofread for Spelling

**Proofread Bert's story. Circle the eight misspelled words.
Then write the correct spellings on the lines below.**

Last week we went to visit my Grandpa's farm. I couldn't wait, but my dad kept driving slowlee! When we finally arrived, Grandpa took me to the barn.

In the corner of a pen, I saw a goat breathing weakely. Saddly, Grandpa said it was sick. The vet gave the goat some pills. The goat ate them with a mothful of corn. Grandpa was hopful that the goat would get well. I stayed safly out of the pen. It would be paynful if the goat kicked me.

After dinner, Grandpa and I went to check on the goat. It was running around in its pen! Grandpa and I were happy and tankful that the goat was feeling better.

Spelling Words

**Basic
Words**
1. helpful
2. sadly
3. hopeful
4. thankful
5. slowly
6. wishful
7. kindly
8. useful
9. safely
10. painful
11. mouthful
12. weakly

1. _____ 5. _____

2. _____ 8. _____

3. _____ 7. _____

4. _____ 8. _____

Forms of the Verb *be*

Circle the correct form of the verb *be*. Then rewrite the sentence on the line below.

1. The women (are, is) weavers.

_____

2. The wool (is, were) soft.

_____

3. The rugs (were, was) pretty.

_____

4. We (are, is) interested in rugs.

_____

5. I (am, is) in a rug store.

_____

6. It (is, are) a new rug.

_____

7. That (are, is) the one I want.

_____

8. The other rugs (was, were) too large.

_____

125

Conventions

Wrong	Right
We <u>has</u> a new rug.	We <u>have</u> a new rug.

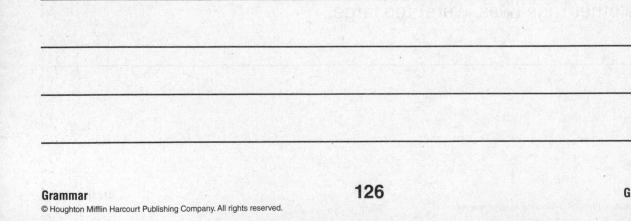 **Read the paragraphs. Find six verb mistakes. Then rewrite each sentence. Make sure each verb matches the subject in the sentence.**

Sue Makes Rugs

Sue have a loom now. She likes to weave rugs. We has a rug from her now. I watch Sue work. She do a lot to get ready to weave.

Last week, Sue needed wool. Yesterday, Sue do a trade with the owner of the wool store. Now the owner have a rug, too. Now Sue have enough wool for many rugs!

_____

_____

_____

_____

_____

_____

_____

Prefixes

Make words with prefixes. Read the base word.
Then add the prefix at the top of the column and
write the new word.

	un-	**re-**
1. lock	_____	_____
2. tie	_____	_____
3. pin	_____	_____
4. fold	_____	_____
5. pack	_____	_____

Complete each sentence. Add a prefix from the box to the base
word at the end of the sentence. Write the new word on the line.

over-	**pre-**	**mis-**

6. Set an alarm clock so you do not

_____. **sleep**

7. Before the real test, we will have a

_____. **test**

8. Be careful not to _____

any words. **spell**

Irregular Action Verbs

- *Run, come, sit, hide,* and *tell* are **irregular verbs**. You do not add an *-ed* ending to these verbs to tell about the past.

Thinking Question
Is the action happening now or did it happen in the past?

Happening Now	Happened in the Past
The ducks **come** to the pond.	The ducks **came** to the pond.
The chipmunks **run** away.	The chipmunks **ran** away.
The pigs **sit** in the mud.	The pigs **sat** in the mud.
The children **hide** in the field.	The children **hid** in the field.
The parents **tell** a story.	The parents **told** a story.

Read and circle the word that tells when the action happens. Write each sentence using the correct verb.

1. The cows (come, came) from the fields.   **now**

_____

2. The children (run, ran) down the path.   **now**

_____

3. They (sit, sat) in the field.   **past**

_____

4. They all (hide, hid) in the dark.   **past**

_____

Prefixes

Read each word. Then write the prefix and base word on the lines.

1. unsafe _____   _____

2. recheck _____   _____

3. retell _____   _____

4. overeat _____   _____

5. unwise _____   _____

6. repaint _____   _____

Add the prefix *re-, mis-,* or *pre-* to the base word at the end of each sentence. Write the new word on the line to complete the sentence.

7. I _____ the oven before

I bake. **heat**

8. I listen carefully so I won't

_____. **understand**

9. I will study again and _____

the test. **take**

Half-Chicken
Spelling: Prefixes *re-* and *un-*

Prefixes *re-* and *un-*

Sort the Basic Words by the prefixes *re-* and *un-*.
Underline the prefix in each word.

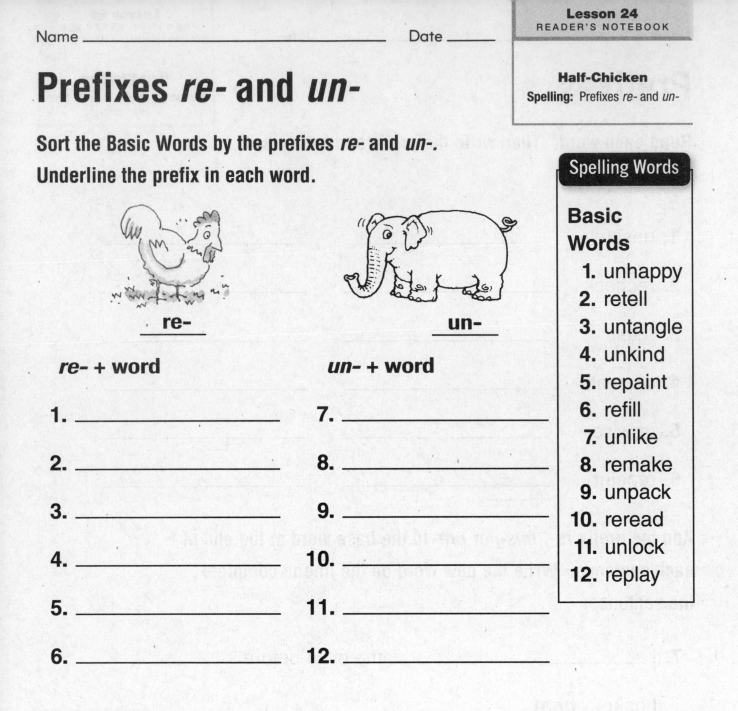

___re-   ___un-

re- + word   **un- + word**

1. _____   7. _____

2. _____   8. _____

3. _____   9. _____

4. _____   10. _____

5. _____   11. _____

6. _____   12. _____

Spelling Words
Basic Words
1. unhappy
2. retell
3. untangle
4. unkind
5. repaint
6. refill
7. unlike
8. remake
9. unpack
10. reread
11. unlock
12. replay

See, Saw and Go, Went

- *See* and *go* are **irregular verbs**. Do not add an *-ed* ending to these verbs to tell about the past.
- *See* tells about an action happening now. *Saw* tells about an action in the past.
- *Go* tells about an action happening now. *Went* tells about an action in the past.

Thinking Question
Is the action happening now or did it happen in the past?

Happening Now	Happened in the Past
The squirrels **go** up a tree.	The squirrels **went** up a tree.
The squirrels **see** their food.	The squirrels **saw** their food.

Read the word that tells when the action happens. Write each sentence using the correct verb.

1. The chicks (see, saw) their mother.   **now**

_____

2. The chicks (go, went) with their mother.   **now**

_____

3. All of the chickens (see, saw) the chicks.   **past**

_____

4. The chickens (go, went) quickly to their nests.   **past**

_____

Focus Trait: Ideas
Exact Details

Sentence	Sentence with Exact Details
Animals live on this ranch.	**Horses, pigs, chickens, and cows** live on this ranch.

A. Read each sentence. Add exact details to make each sentence clearer and more interesting.

Sentence	Sentence with Exact Details
1. The hen ate.	The _____ hen _____
2. The chicks gathered around their mother.	The _____ chicks gathered around their mother _____ _____

B. Read each sentence. Look at the picture on pages 320–321 of *Half-Chicken*. Add exact details to make each sentence clearer.

Sentence	Sentence with Exact Details
3. Everyone came to see.	
4. Plants grew in the field.	

132

Silent Consonants

Write a word from the sentence to answer the question.

1. Would you **kneel** or **knit** a hat? _____

2. Would you **crumb** or **climb** a hill? _____

3. Would you **knob** or **knock** on a door? _____

4. Could you bend a **wrong** or a **wrist**? _____

5. Would you tie a **knot** or a **knife**? _____

6. Is a **gnat** or a **gnu** very small? _____

7. Would a **comb** or a **lamb** eat grass? _____

8. Would you **wrench** or **wrap** a gift? _____

Use words from above to write two new sentences.

9. _____

10. _____

Reader's Guide

Half-Chicken

Draw and Label a Picture

This story tells about a very special chicken and his trip to Mexico City. Reread pages from the story and write what happened at each part of the trip.

Read page 321. Why does Half-Chicken decide to go on a trip?

_____

_____

Read pages 323–324. Who does he help along the way?

_____

_____

Read pages 327–329. What happens in the viceroy's court?

_____

_____

Read pages 330–331. Where does Half-Chicken end up staying?

_____

_____

Half-Chicken wants to send a postcard to his family. Draw a picture on the front. Tell the story of Half-Chicken's adventure on the back.

Front

Back

Dear Family,

_____

_____

_____

_____

_____

_____

_____

Mrs. Chicken and Family

The Ranch

Countryside, Mexico City

Prefixes *re-* and *un-*

Write the Basic Word that matches each meaning.

1. fill again _____

2. tell again _____

3. read again _____

4. play again _____

5. make again _____

6. paint again _____

7. not happy _____

8. not like _____

9. not kind _____

10. undo a lock _____

Spelling Words

Basic Words

1. unhappy
2. retell
3. untangle
4. unkind
5. repaint
6. refill
7. unlike
8. remake
9. unpack
10. reread
11. unlock
12. replay

Irregular Action Verbs

Read the word that tells when the action happens.
Then write each sentence using the correct verb.

1. The horses (hide, hid) with their babies.   **now**

   _____

2. The colts (come, came) to the water.   **now**

   _____

3. The animals (run, ran) for a drink.   **past**

   _____

4. The boys (see, saw) the horses.   **past**

   _____

5. The girls (go, went) to the barn.   **past**

   _____

6. The dogs (sit, sat) with the girls.   **now**

   _____

7. The girls (tell, told) the boys where to go.   **past**

   _____

Name _____ Date _____

Lesson 24
READER'S NOTEBOOK

Half-Chicken
Vocabulary Strategies:
Antonyms

Antonyms

Circle the two words that are antonyms in each sentence.

1. James put his wet shirt in the sun so it would get dry.

2. Cindy put the soft pillow on the hard chair.

3. Nathan filled a tall glass with water and sat down to do his short paper.

4. Amy used her strong arms to pull down the weak and broken branches of the tree.

Circle the two words in each group that are antonyms.

5.   swift   steady   slow

6.   high   full   empty

7.   cold   hot   cloudy

8.   sunny   hilly   cloudy

9.   before   over   under

10. smooth   bumpy   brush

138
Grade 2, Unit 5

Proofread for Spelling

Proofread the newspaper article. Circle the eight misspelled words. Then write the correct spellings on the lines below.

Spelling Words

Basic Words

1. unhappy
2. retell
3. untangle
4. unkind
5. repaint
6. refill
7. unlike
8. remake
9. unpack
10. reread
11. unlock
12. replay

New at the Ranch

The Wild Bill Ranch is getting a new prize bull named Ollie.

This morning, ranch hands arrived to unpak a huge crate. Out came a very unhapi bull.

"It might seem unkined to put Ollie in a crate," said the rancher. "But it was the best way to keep him safe. Once we unlok the crate and untanglel Ollie from his blanket, he will soon forget about it. Ollie's ncw space is unlik the small pen he once called home."

Watch tonight's news to see a repla of Ollie's arrival. You can buy the book that reteels Ollie's story.

1. _____   5. _____

2. _____   6. _____

3. _____   7. _____

4. _____   8. _____

Commas in Dates and Places

Read each sentence. Rewrite each date or place. Put the comma in the correct place.

1. We visited Mexico on June 17 2011.

_____

2. I came from Atlanta Georgia.

_____

3. We saw horses on June 20 2011.

_____

4. Later, I visited Chicago Illinois.

_____

5. The baby elephant was born on April, 2 2012.

_____

6. I heard the story in Miami Florida.

_____

7. I took a plane to Los Angeles California.

_____

8. I saw ten chicks on May 1 2012.

_____

Word Choice:
Using Exact Verbs

Without Exact Verb	With Exact Verb
The lions <u>move</u> quickly	The lions <u>dash</u> quickly.

Replace each underlined word with an exact word from the box. Write the new sentences. Underline the exact words.

race	hurt	watched	hid	squawks

1. Yesterday, I <u>saw</u> a fox.

_____

2. I saw the fox <u>move</u> past our barn.

_____

3. The chickens made many <u>noises</u>.

_____

4. Finally, they <u>sat</u> in their nests.

_____

5. They thought the fox would <u>bother</u> them.

_____

Name _____ Date _____

Lesson 25
READER'S NOTEBOOK

From Seed to Plant
Phonics: Words with *au*, *aw*,
al, *o*, *a*

Words with *au*, *aw*, *al*, *o*, *a*

Complete the puzzle with words that have the vowel
sound you hear in *saw*.

Read each clue. Then choose a word from the box.

Word Bank

toss	straw	tall	paw	salt
frost	pause	lost	soft	lawn

ACROSS

1. a dog's foot

2. cannot find

5. something to sip through

6. throw

8. gives food flavor

DOWN

1. a quick stop

2. grass

3. not short

4. icy coating

7. not hard

Say, Said and Eat, Ate

- The verbs *say* and *eat* are **irregular verbs**.
- *Say* tells about an action happening now.
  Said tells about an action in the past.
- *Eat* tells about an action happening now.
  Ate tells about an action in the past.

Happening Now	Happened in the Past
The rabbits **say** they are hungry now.	Then the rabbits **said** they were hungry.
Today, the rabbits **eat** lunch.	The rabbits **ate** lunch yesterday.

Thinking Question
Is the action happening now or did it happen in the past?

Read each sentence. Underline the correct verb. Then rewrite each sentence using the correct verb.

1. Yesterday, the rabbits (eat, ate) carrots.   **past**

_____

2. They (say, said) that they were still hungry.   **past**

_____

3. Today, they (eat, ate) tomatoes.   **now**

_____

4. Now the rabbits (say, said) they are still hungry. **now**

_____

Lesson 25
READER'S NOTEBOOK

From Seed to Plant
Phonics: Words with *au, aw,*
al, o, a

Words with *au, aw,* *al, o, a*

In each row, circle the words that have the /aw/ sound as in *saw*.

1. flaw   hog   some   ball   soft

2. talk   cold   drawn   hang   launch

3. smoke   salt   small   faucet   off

4. toss   awful   cane   pale   water

5. mall   chalk   jaw   autumn   yawn

Circle the word that completes the sentence and write it on the line.

6. Paul and I went for a _____.
   frost   walk

7. A _____ sat on a high branch.
   haul   hawk

8. I saw its sharp _____.
   claws   clogs

Words with *aw, al, o*

Sort the Spelling Words by the */aw/* sound spelled
al, aw, and *o.*

| al | aw | o |

al words	**aw words**	**o words**
1. _____	8. _____	12. _____
2. _____	9. _____	13. _____
3. _____	10. _____	14. _____
4. _____	11. _____	
5. _____		
6. _____		
7. _____		

Spelling Words

Basic Words
1. tall
2. saw
3. dog
4. draw
5. call
6. fall
7. soft
8. paw
9. ball
10. yawn
11. log
12. small

Review Words
13. all
14. walk

Give, Gave and Take, Took

- The verbs *give* and *take* are **irregular verbs**.
- *Give* tells about an action happening now.
  Gave tells about an action in the past.
- *Take* tells about an action happening now.
  Took tells about an action in the past.

Happening Now	Happened in the Past
They **give** the gardener seeds now.	Last fall they **gave** the gardener seeds.
They **take** the vegetables home now.	They **took** the vegetables home yesterday.

Thinking Question
Is the action happening now or did it happen in the past?

Read each sentence. Underline the correct verb. Then rewrite each sentence using the correct verb.

1. Last year, the children (give, gave) me seeds.   **past**

_____

2. I (take, took) the seeds to my garden last spring.   **past**

_____

3. All that summer, I (give, gave) the plants water.   **past**

_____

4. Now I (take, took) vegetables from my garden.   **now**

_____

Focus Trait: Voice
Using Your Own Words

Original Sentences	Writer's Own Words
Plants such as pumpkins, zucchini, yellow squash, and sunflowers grow very big. Their seeds need to be planted far apart to give them room to grow.	Some plants are very big. They need extra room to grow. Be careful not to plant their seeds close together.

Read each original sentence or set of sentences. Paraphrase each by using different words to give the same information.

Original Sentences	Your Own Words
1. Sometimes it is hard to find potatoes in a garden because they grow underground.	
2. Rabbits eat only plants. They use their long ears to listen for animals that might eat them.	
3. Bees and butterflies carry pollen from flower to flower.	
4. Some scientists believe the tomato first came from Mexico.	
5. Thousands of types of apples exist.	

Cumulative Review

Read each question. Make a word that answers each question by choosing a word from the box and adding the suffix *-y, -ly,* or *-ful* to it.

Word Bank

hand	rock	neat
skill	bump	

Which word describes . . .

1. a place with rocks? _____

2. someone with a skill? _____

3. working in a neat way? _____

4. an amount held in a hand? _____

5. a road with bumps? _____

Add *-y, -ly,* or *-ful* to the word in bold print so that the sentence makes sense.

6. The kitten is very **play**. _____

7. She walks **soft** across the tile. _____

8. She gets **sleep** in the daytime. _____

Reader's Guide

From Seed to Plant

Scientist's Notebook

Be a scientist! Study growing plants to see what happens. Take notes and make sketches in your research log.

Read pages 352–353.

Describe what happens.

_____

_____

_____

_____

_____

_____

_____

_____

_____

Read pages 354–356.

Describe what happens.

_____

_____

_____

_____

_____

_____

Read pages 359–360.

Describe what happens.

_____

_____

_____

_____

_____

_____

Words with *aw, al, o*

Write the Spelling Word that belongs in each group.

1. wood, tree, _____

2. foot, hoof, _____

3. cat, bird, _____

4. heard, touched, _____

5. paint, sketch, _____

6. bat, glove, _____

7. summer, winter, _____

8. shout, yell, _____

9. sleep, snore, _____

Spelling Words
Basic Words
1. tall
2. saw
3. dog
4. draw
5. call
6. fall
7. soft
8. paw
9. ball
10. yawn
11. log
12. small
Review Words
13. all
14. walk

Write the Spelling Word that is the opposite of the given word.

10. hard _____

11. short _____

12. none _____

13. run _____

14. large _____

More Irregular Action Verbs

✏ **Read each sentence. Use the clue and underline the correct verb. Then rewrite each sentence using the correct verb that tells about now or the past.**

1. The farmers (say, said) they planted corn.   **past**

_____

2. Today, the children (eat, ate) a lot of corn.   **now**

_____

3. The farmers (say, said) they can bring more corn.   **now**

_____

4. We (give, gave) vegetables to our friends.   **past**

_____

5. They (give, gave) us fruit from their trees.   **now**

_____

6. We (take, took) two apples from the basket.   **now**

_____

Using Context

Use clues in the sentence to find the meaning of the
underlined word. Then find the word's meaning in the
box. Write the definition on the line.

┌─────────────────── Word Bank ───────────────────┐

something that helps plants grow   move quickly
        take small bites   speak with anger
   someone who lives nearby   lucky

└──┘

1. I like to <u>nibble</u> the carrot. I eat it like a bunny.

_____

2. Lisa is very late. She has to <u>rush</u> to catch the school

bus. _____

3. Please don't <u>scold</u> me. I did not mean to drop the

cup. _____

4. Jake is our <u>neighbor</u>. He walks to my house to play.

_____

5. Dad uses <u>fertilizer</u> in the garden. He wants the plants

to be healthy. _____

6. My sister has the flu. I feel very <u>fortunate</u> that I

didn't catch it. _____

Proofread for Spelling

Proofread this journal entry. Circle the eight misspelled words. Then write the correct spellings on the lines below.

April 10, 2010

    I think spring is here. Today I sow a robin. I have not seen one since last fal. I like spring because I spend more time outside.

    I like to plant seeds in the sawft mud of Mom's flower garden. Then I drow pictures of the flowers on smoll cards and place the signs at the head of each row.

    My dog Max likes to help, but just one paw can smash my plants. Mom will call him away to chase his ball. Sometimes Max will just sit near me and yown in the sun.

    Soon my plants will grow toll. Then I will sit on a lawg and smell my flowers.

Spelling Words

Basic Words

1. tall
2. saw
3. dog
4. draw
5. call
6. fall
7. soft
8. paw
9. ball
10. yawn
11. log
12. small

1. _____ 5. _____

2. _____ 6. _____

3. _____ 7. _____

4. _____ 8. _____

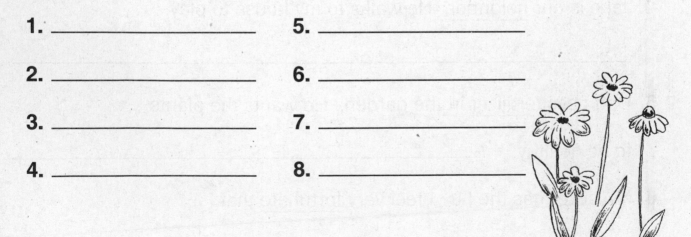

Commas in a Series

Draw a line under each correct sentence.

1. Mom's garden has tomatoes, peppers and squash.

   Mom's garden has tomatoes, peppers, and squash.

2. She planted on Sunday, Monday, and Tuesday.

   She planted, on Sunday Monday and Tuesday.

3. We helped her dig plant, and water.

   We helped her dig, plant, and water.

4. I planted the carrots celery and eggplant.

   I planted the carrots, celery, and eggplant.

5. We saw, bees, birds and butterflies on the plants.

   We saw bees, birds, and butterflies on the plants.

6. We will have vegetables in June, July, and August.

   We will have vegetables in, June July and, August.

Sentence Fluency

Incorrect

Last week she **gives** me a bag of carrots.

I **taked** the carrots home.

Correct

Last week she **gave** me a bag of carrots.

I **took** the carrots home.

Read this story about last summer. Write the paragraph correctly. Change each underlined verb to tell about the past.

My Summer Garden

Last year, I grew a garden. I take seeds and put them in the ground. I gived them water. Mom and Dad say we could pick the vegetables when they grow. Soon, the garden grew. I give eggplant to Mom. I take carrots for myself. We eat it all. Yum!

_____

_____

_____

_____

Words with *oo, ew, ue, ou*

Put these letters together to write words with the vowel sound you hear in *zoo*.

1. m + oo + n _____

2. s + ou + p _____

3. c + h + ew _____

4. b + l + ue _____

5. p + oo + l _____

Now use the words you wrote above to complete the sentences below.

6. Did you see the _____ and the stars last night?

7. We swim in the _____.

8. I ate a bowl of hot _____.

9. The sun is shining in the _____ sky.

10. Our puppy likes to _____ on socks.

The Mysterious Tadpole
Grammar: Contractions

Contractions with *not*

- A **contraction** is a short way of writing two words.
- An **apostrophe (')** shows where letters were left out.

Thinking Question
Which two words are being put together to make a contraction?

Two Words	Contraction
do not	**don't**
does not	**doesn't**
is not	**isn't**
cannot	**can't**

Write contractions for the underlined words.

1. I <u>do not</u> believe my eyes! _____

2. Your pet <u>is not</u> friendly. _____

3. I <u>cannot</u> believe your pig can fly. _____

4. Your pig <u>does not</u> have wings. _____

5. I <u>do not</u> know how it can fly! _____

6. Our art teacher <u>does not</u> come on Tuesdays.

_____

Words with *oo, ew, ue, ou*

The Mysterious Tadpole
Phonics: Words with *oo, ew, ue, ou*

Answer each pair of clues using the words below the clues.

1. Something that helps solve a mystery _____

The people who work on a ship _____

crew **clue**

2. To move quickly _____

A place to see animals _____

zoom **zoo**

3. Many people together _____

Got bigger _____

group **grew**

4. Lift or push someone from below _____

In a little while _____

soon **boost**

5. Moved by using wings _____

Not many _____

flew **few**

Name _____ Date _____

Words with *oo (ew, oo, ou)*

The Mysterious Tadpole
Spelling: Words with *oo*
(*ew, oo, ou*)

Sort the words by the spelling for the vowel sound in *moon*.

With *oo* | **With *ew*** | **With *ou***

1. _____

2. _____

3. _____

4. _____

5. _____

6. _____

7. _____

8. _____

9. _____

10. _____

11. _____

12. _____

13. _____

14. _____

Underline the letters in each word that make the vowel sound in *moon*.

Spelling Words

Basic Words

1. root
2. crew
3. spoon
4. few
5. bloom
6. grew
7. room
8. you
9. stew
10. boost
11. scoop
12. flew

Review Words

13. zoo
14. noon

Contractions with Pronouns

- A **contraction** is a word made by putting two words together.
- An **apostrophe** replaces the letter or letters that were left out.
- Many contractions are made by joining a **pronoun** and a **verb.**

Two Words	Contraction
I am	I'm
You will	You'll
She will	She'll
We are	We're
They are	They're
She is	She's
It is	It's

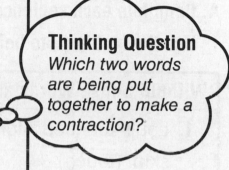

Thinking Question
Which two words are being put together to make a contraction?

✏ **Write contractions for the underlined words.**

1. I am surprised to see a pink tadpole. _____

2. They are supposed to be brown. _____

3. It is a funny looking creature. _____

4. We are not sure why it is so big. _____

5. You will wonder about this strange pet. _____

Focus Trait: Word Choice
Sense Words and Details

The Mysterious Tadpole
Writing: Opinion Writing

Without Sense Words and Details	With Sense Words and Details
Louis saw a tadpole.	Louis saw a **huge spotted** tadpole.

A. Complete each sentence, using sense words and details.

Use the hint in ( ) to help you.

Without Sense Words and Details	With Sense Words and Details
1. Louis touched Alphonse's skin. (touch)	Louis touched Alphonse's _____ skin.
2. Louis smelled the water. (smell)	Louis smelled the _____ water.

B. Read each weak sentence. Rewrite each sentence.

Add sense words and details.

Pair/Share Work with a partner to brainstorm powerful words.

Weak Language	Powerful Language
3. Alphonse ate a snack.	
4. Louis heard a sound.	

Cumulative Review

Add the suffix *-y*, *-ly*, or *-ful* to each word. Write the word on the line and read each completed sentence.

1. rain: I painted my bedroom one

_____ day.

2. slow: I painted _____.

3. care: I was _____ not to spill.

4. hope: Mom was _____ that I

would finish by noon.

5. quick: I tried painting _____.

6. mess: It was _____.

Add the prefix to each base word. Then write the new word on the line.

7. re + paint = _____

8. un + cover = _____

9. over + look = _____

10. pre + mix = _____

11. mis + match = _____

Reader's Guide

The Mysterious Tadpole

Write a Letter

Hi. I'm Louis. My uncle gave me a pet. Use the text and illustrations to help me write letters about my amazing pet!

Read pages 386–387. Then write a letter from Louis to Uncle McAllister.

Dear Uncle McAllister,

_____

_____

_____

Love, Louis

Read pages 388 and 391. Then write another letter to Uncle McAllister. What happened since your last letter?

Dear Uncle McAllister,

_____

_____

Love, Louis

Read pages 397–399. Write another letter from Louis to Uncle McAllister. Let him know what happened on these pages.

Dear Uncle McAllister,

_____

_____

_____

_____

Love, Louis

Read pages 400–402. What happens in this part of the story? Use what you read to write another letter from Louis to Uncle McAllister.

Dear Uncle McAllister,

_____

_____

_____

_____

Love, Louis

Words with *oo (ew, oo, ou)*

The Mysterious Tadpole
Spelling: Words with *oo*
(*ew, oo, ou*)

Write the Spelling Word that matches each meaning.

1. not many _____

2. got bigger _____

3. animal park _____

4. raise _____

5. midday _____

6. pick up _____

Write the Basic Word that belongs in each group.

7. glided, floated, _____

8. team, helpers, _____

9. knife, fork, _____

10. chowder, chili, _____

11. kitchen, den, _____

12. flower, open, _____

13. tree, trunk, _____

14. me, us, _____

Spelling Words

Basic Words

1. root
2. crew
3. spoon
4. few
5. bloom
6. grew
7. room
8. you
9. stew
10. boost
11. scoop
12. flew

Review Words

13. zoo
14. noon

Contractions

Write the contraction for each underlined word or words.

1. Tina knows that cats <u>do not</u> talk. _____

2. She <u>is not</u> sure why her cat can sing. _____

3. Tina <u>cannot</u> tell people about the cat. _____

4. She <u>does not</u> think anyone will believe her.

_____

Write each sentence. Write a contraction in place of the underlined words.

5. <u>We are</u> tadpoles in a pond.

_____

6. <u>They are</u> afraid of us.

_____

7. <u>You will</u> see that <u>I am</u> small.

_____

8. But <u>I am</u> going to be ten feet tall!

_____

Multiple-Meaning Words

Read the words and their definitions. Decide which meaning fits the underlined word in each sentence below. Write the correct definition on the line.

fly	1. a small insect with wings
	2. to move through the air like a bird or insect
line	1. a number of people or things in a row
	2. a long piece of string or wire used for fishing
upset	1. unhappy or disappointed about something
	2. to turn, tip, or knock something over

1. Ed used a worm as bait on his fishing <u>line</u>.

_____

2. Sasha got <u>upset</u> when she heard the bad news.

_____

3. The kids waited in <u>line</u> to get a drink of water.

_____

4. An eagle can <u>fly</u> for many miles.

_____

5. The <u>fly</u> was buzzing around the picnic table.

_____

Proofread for Spelling

The Mysterious Tadpole
Spelling: Words with *oo*
(*ew, oo, ou*)

**Proofread the paragraphs. Circle the eight misspelled words.
Then write the correct spellings on the lines below.**

Spelling Words
1. root
2. crew
3. spoon
4. few
5. bloom
6. grew
7. room
8. you
9. stew
10. boost
11. scoop
12. flew

Do yoo have a plant? When I groo up, I had a plant in my ruem. It was a pretty little tree. It grew inside a pot. Its rewts were deep.

I fed the plant every month. I gave it a fou scups of plant food. In the summer, I would bewst it up to the window so it could get more sun. Once a year, it grew beautiful red bloums.

1. _____   5. _____

2. _____   6. _____

3. _____   7. _____

4. _____   8. _____

Write these other Spelling Words in ABC order: *crew, spoon,
stew, flew.*

9. _____   11. _____

10. _____   12. _____

Kinds of Adjectives

✎ **Circle the adjective that best completes the sentence.**
Use the clue at the end of the sentence.

1. The tadpoles are (big, brown). (color)

2. There are (forty, long) of them. (how many)

3. They are (tall, slippery). (feel)

4. They are (tiny, angry). (size)

✎ **Read each pair of sentences. Join the sentences using**
and between the two adjectives. Write the new sentence.

5. The ocean water was deep.

The ocean water was cold.

_____

6. The fish were happy.

The fish were surprised.

_____

Contractions

Incorrect	Correct
The mysterious horse <u>is'nt</u> growing.	The mysterious horse <u>isn't</u> growing.
<u>H'es</u> getting smaller!	<u>He's</u> getting smaller!

Read the paragraph. Circle five mistakes with contractions. Copy the story and write the contractions correctly.

The Mysterious Horse

Im' going to tell you a story. I once knew a pony named Lou. He was'nt a big pony. And he did'nt get any bigger, either. One day he started to shrink. H'es still getting smaller today. I think one day hel'l be the smallest horse in the world!

_____

_____

_____

_____

_____

Name _____ Date _____

Words with *oo* as in *book*

Word Bank

cookbook   cook   took
good   cookies   looking

Write a word from the box to complete each sentence. Then read each completed sentence.

1. My father and I like to _____.

2. Last Saturday I was _____

for something to do.

3. "Let's bake oatmeal _____,"

said Dad.

4. We followed all the steps in the _____.

5. Mom _____ one of our treats.

6. She agreed that they tasted _____.

Write two rhyming words for each word below.

cook   **good**

_____   _____

_____   _____

Adverbs That Tell How

- An **adverb** describes a verb.

- **Adverbs** can tell about how something is done.

We lined up <u>quickly</u>.
We got off the bus <u>slowly</u>.

Thinking Questions
Which word tells how the action was done?

Read each sentence. Think about the action. Then underline the adverb that tells how the action was done.

1. The bus driver spoke loudly.

2. He carefully called each name.

3. She raised her hand shyly.

4. He nicely helped her climb the steps.

5. They got to the museum quickly.

6. Quietly, the children asked questions.

7. They looked at the dinosaurs together.

8. Then they talked softly.

Words with *oo* as in *book*

Word Bank

brook	hoof	hook	good	football
look	wood	foot	woof	cookies

Read the words below. Think about how the words in each group are alike. Then choose an *oo* word from the box that goes with each group. Write the word on the line.

1. hand, eye, _____

2. kickball, baseball, _____

3. nice, fine, _____

4. mane, tail, _____

5. moo, chirp, _____

6. creek, stream, _____

7. pies, cakes, _____

8. see, peek, _____

9. brick, glass, _____

10. bait, pole, _____

Words with *oo* as in *book*

Sort the Spelling Words by final consonants.

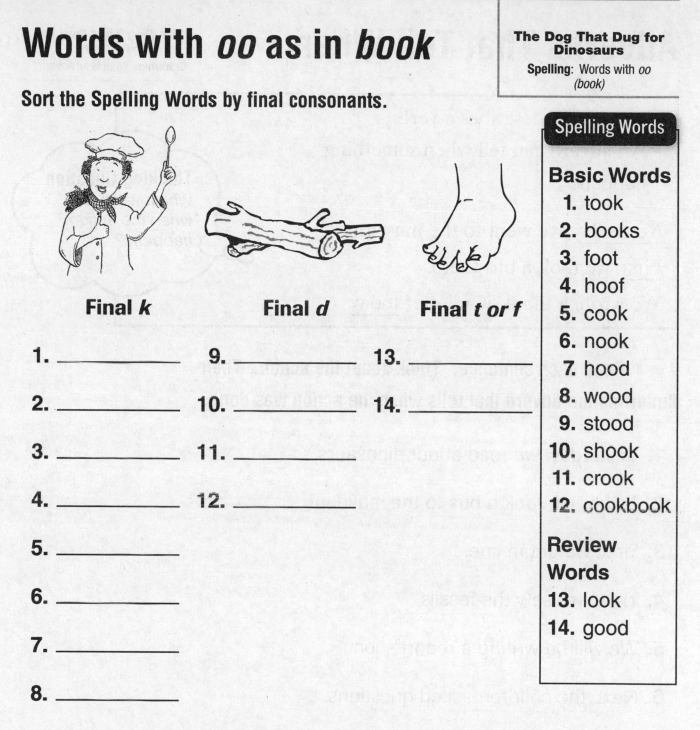

Final *k*	**Final *d***	**Final *t or f***
1. _____	9. _____	13. _____
2. _____	10. _____	14. _____
3. _____	11. _____	
4. _____	12. _____	
5. _____		
6. _____		
7. _____		
8. _____		

Spelling Words

Basic Words
1. took
2. books
3. foot
4. hoof
5. cook
6. nook
7. hood
8. wood
9. stood
10. shook
11. crook
12. cookbook

Review Words
13. look
14. good

Name _____ Date _____

Lesson 27
READER'S NOTEBOOK

The Dog That Dug for Dinosaurs
Grammar: What Is an Adverb?

Adverbs That Tell When

- An **adverb** describes a verb.
- An **adverb** can tell when something happens.

Yesterday, we went to the museum.

First, we took a bus there.

We wrote a thank-you letter today.

Thinking Question
Which word tells when the action happens?

✏️ **Read each sentence. Think about the action. Then underline the adverb that tells when the action was done.**

1. Yesterday, we read about dinosaurs.

2. Today, we took a bus to the museum.

3. First, we got in line.

4. Then, we saw the fossils.

5. We will be writing a report soon.

6. Next, the children asked questions.

7. They looked at the dinosaurs later.

8. Then, they talked on the bus.

Focus Trait: Organization Introduction and Conclusion

The **introduction sentence** of a book report tells about the book and gives an opinion about the book.

Sentences that give **reasons** tell facts to support the opinion.

The **conclusion sentence** sums up the information and tells the opinion in a different way.

Label the introduction sentence, the sentences that give reasons, and the conclusion sentence.

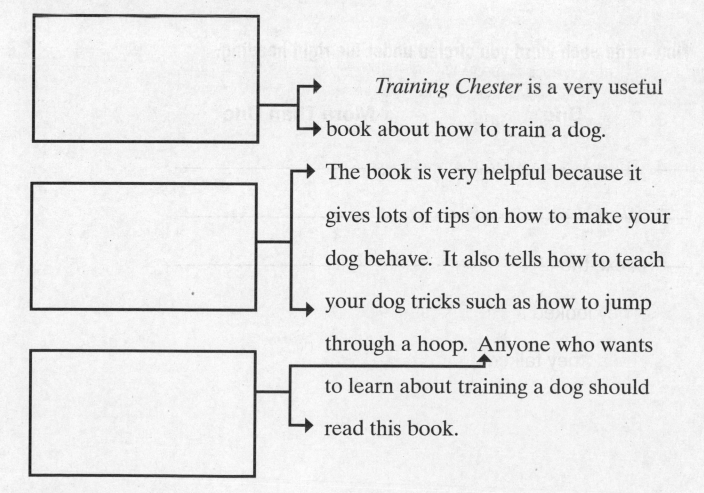

Training Chester is a very useful book about how to train a dog.

The book is very helpful because it gives lots of tips on how to make your dog behave. It also tells how to teach your dog tricks such as how to jump through a hoop. Anyone who wants to learn about training a dog should read this book.

Possessive Nouns

Read the sentences. Draw a circle around each word that shows who or what owns something.

1. The bike's tire is flat.

2. We laughed at the seals' tricks.

3. The ladies' club has a meeting today.

4. The little rabbit's tail is white and fluffy.

5. The book's pages are torn.

6. The girls' team has a game on Thursday.

Now write each word you circled under the right heading.

One	More Than One
_____	_____
_____	_____
_____	_____

Name _____ Date _____

Lesson 27
READER'S NOTEBOOK

**The Dog That Dug
for Dinosaurs**
Independent Reading

Reader's Guide

The Dog That Dug for Dinosaurs

Create a Fossil Hunting Guide

Use the text and illustrations to help Digger
complete a fossil hunting guide.

Read pages 425–426.

**Describe fossils and
the tools needed to find them.**

Read pages 427–428.

Explain to readers how to find fossils.

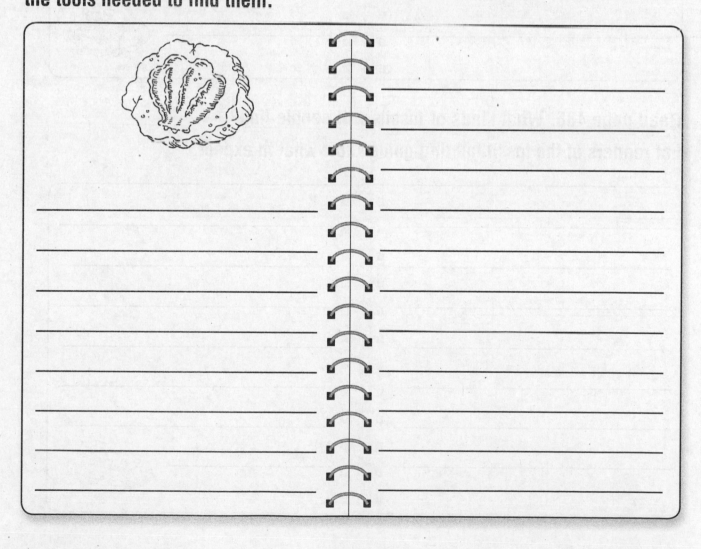

Name _____ Date _____

Lesson 27
READER'S NOTEBOOK

**The Dog That Dug
for Dinosaurs**
Independent Reading

**Read pages 434–435. Keep writing your fossil hunting
guide. Tell your readers about some of the dangers
of fossil hunting.**

Read page 436. What kinds of fossils will people find?
Let readers of the fossil hunting guide know what to expect.

Words with *oo* as in *book*

Write the Basic Word that matches each clue.

Spelling Words

Basic Words
1. took
2. books
3. foot
4. hoof
5. cook
6. nook
7. hood
8. wood
9. stood
10. shook
11. crook
12. cookbook

1. Opposite of gave _____

2. To make food _____

3. Part of a coat that covers your head

_____

4. Things you read _____

5. A cow stands on this, but you don't.

_____

6. A small place to sit _____

7. Got up from sitting _____

8. You put a shoe over this.

_____

9. A book used to make food

_____

10. It comes from trees. _____

11. A person who steals _____

12. Wiggled all over _____

Name _____ Date _____

Lesson 27
READER'S NOTEBOOK

The Dog That Dug for
Dinosaurs
Grammar: What Is an Adverb?

Adverbs and Adjectives

Draw a line under the adverb that tells how or when.

1. Yesterday, we saw a show about dinosaurs.

2. We went there together.

3. We listened carefully to all the facts.

4. We took notes quietly.

5. Today, we are talking about the show.

6. Our teacher quickly lists the facts.

7. Tomorrow, we will write our papers.

8. Then, we will share our reports.

9. We will speak clearly.

10. The others will listen politely.

Choose the adverb or adjective that best completes
each sentence. Underline it.

11. We watched the dog run (quickly, quick) to the dirt area.

12. He was (careful, carefully) while digging for the old bones.

Name _____ Date _____

Lesson 27
READER'S NOTEBOOK

The Dog That Dug for
Dinosaurs
Vocabulary Strategies:
Shades of Meaning

Shades of Meaning

**Read the story. Complete each sentence by writing
the word that fits better.**

Tina and Larry went on a hike. They stopped at a creek

to _____ their lunch. Tina took her boots off.
  (eat   gobble)

She put her feet in the creek. "This feels good," she said. "The

water is _____."
  (freezing   cool)

"Look at that _____ animal," said
  (tiny   small)

Larry. "It's the size of a mouse. I think it's a chipmunk." He

_____ a peanut and tossed it to the chipmunk.
  (broke   smashed)

From the top of a hill, the children _____
  (saw   spotted)

another hiker. "Hey," said Tina, "that's Rob. He likes to hike

too." She _____ to get Rob's attention. Soon
  (screamed   yelled)

the three friends were hiking together.

"We should turn around," said Lawrence. "I'm

_____ we might not get home in time for dinner.
  (worried   scared)

I'm starving. I want to eat a _____ hamburger."
  (large   giant)

Proofread for Spelling

**Proofread the story. Circle the eight misspelled words.
Then write the correct spellings on the lines below.**

Spelling Words

I had a funny dream. I dreamed I was sitting in a nook next to an old fireplace. I could smell the wud fire. Near the door, stud a huge cook. I knew because he wore an apron and held a cookbuck.

He came over and shok my hand. Then he pulled a hood over his head and started cooking breakfast. It smelled gud. I saw that his right foat was not in a shoe, but was a huf! He smiled at me. He looked like a character from one of my story boaks!

1. took
2. books
3. foot
4. hoof
5. cook
6. nook
7. hood
8. wood
9. stood
10. shook
11. crook
12. cookbook

Review Words
13. look
14. good

1. _____ 5. _____

2. _____ 6. _____

3. _____ 7. _____

4. _____ 8. _____

Write these other Spelling Words in ABC order: *took, cook, nook, hood, look, crook.*

9. _____ 12. _____

10. _____ 13. _____

11. _____ 14. _____

Name _____ Date _____

Lesson 27
READER'S NOTEBOOK

The Dog That Dug for
Dinosaurs
Grammar: Spiral Review

Using Adjectives

Circle the word that correctly completes the sentence.

1. I found (a, an) fossil today.

2. It is the (bigger, biggest) fossil I have ever seen.

3. It may be (a, an) leg bone of a dinosaur.

4. The other bone I found was (shorter, shortest).

Rewrite the paragraph. Add -er or -est to each underlined adjective. Write the new paragraph on the lines below.

I have the <u>great</u> dog in the world. His name is Chester. Chester digs in the park with his dog friends. Chester is <u>small</u> than his friend Chelsie, but he is the <u>fast</u> of all the dogs. He and his friend Luke find bones. The bone Chester finds is <u>long</u> than the others.

_____

_____

_____

_____

_____

_____

Adverbs

You can combine sentences that describe the same action. Use *and* to join the adverbs.

The tourists walked quickly. The tourists walked quietly.	The tourists walked quickly <u>and</u> quietly.
They are digging today. They are digging tomorrow.	They are digging today <u>and</u> tomorrow.

Read each pair of sentences. Use *and* to join the adverbs and write the new sentence.

1. We read about dinosaurs yesterday.
We read about dinosaurs today.

_____

2. I wrote my notes neatly.
I wrote my notes carefully.

_____

3. I'm going to study today.
I'm going to study tomorrow.

_____

4. I will answer the test questions slowly.
I will answer the test questions correctly.

_____

Words with *ow, ou*

Put these letters together to write words with *ow* and *ou*.
Then read each word aloud.

1. b + ow _____

2. c + l + ow + n _____

3. f + r + ow + n _____

4. l + ou + d _____

5. r + ou + n + d _____

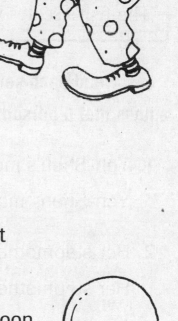

Now use the words you wrote above to complete the
sentences below.

6. Bubbles the _____ came out
   on the stage.

7. He blew up a big _____ balloon.

8. The balloon popped with a
   _____ bang.

9. Bubbles had a big _____ on
   his face.

10. Then Bubbles took a _____
    while the crowd clapped.

Nouns Ending with 's

Yeh-Shen
Grammar: Possessive Nouns

- A **possessive noun** shows that a person, animal, or thing owns or has something.
- When a noun names one person or thing, add an **apostrophe (')** and an **s** to that noun to show ownership. This makes the noun a possessive noun.

The <u>fish's</u> scales were shiny.

Thinking Question
Who or what in the sentence owns or has something?

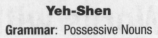

Read each sentence. Underline the sentence that shows that a person owns or has something.

1. Yeh-Shen's mother and father had died.

Yeh-Shens mother and father had died.

2. Her stepmother's cave was cold.

Her stepmothers cave was cold.

3. The old mans advice was helpful.

The old man's advice was helpful.

4. Her friends tail was beautiful.

Her friend's tail was beautiful.

5. The kings men built a hut.

The king's men built a hut.

Words with *ow, ou*

Word Bank

couch	crowd	crown	found	frown
howl	mouth	ouch	round	shout

Write a word from the box that matches each clue.

1. A part of your face _____

2. A sound a dog might make _____

3. A large group of people _____

4. A long seat for sitting _____

5. To yell loudly _____

6. Something a queen has _____

7. The shape of a ball _____

8. The face a grouch makes _____

9. What you say when you get hurt _____

10. Got something you were looking for _____

Words with *ow, ou*

Sort the Spelling Words by the spellings *ow* and *ou*.

Spelling Words

Basic Words
1. cow
2. house
3. town
4. shout
5. down
6. mouse
7. found
8. loud
9. brown
10. ground
11. pound
12. flower

Review Words
13. out
14. now

ow Words

1. _____
2. _____
3. _____
4. _____
5. _____
6. _____

ou Words

7. _____
8. _____
9. _____
10. _____
11. _____
12. _____
13. _____
14. _____

Write the Spelling Words that rhyme with each given word.

15. how, _____, _____

16. blouse, _____, _____

17. clown, _____, _____, _____

18. bound, _____, _____, _____

Nouns Ending with s'

- A **possessive noun** shows that a person, animal, or thing owns or has something.
- When a noun names more than one and ends in **s,** add just an **apostrophe (')** after the **s** to show ownership.

The <u>musicians</u>' show was great.

Thinking Question
Who or what in the sentence owns something?

✏️ **Read each pair of sentences. Underline the sentence that uses a possessive noun correctly.**

1. Her parents death made Yeh-Shen an orphan.

   Her parents' death made Yeh-Shen an orphan.

2. The dancers' costumes were colorful.

   The dancers costumes were colorful.

3. The girls' dresses were beautiful.

   The girls dresses were beautiful.

4. Her admirers praise made her happy.

   Her admirers' praise made her happy.

5. The villagers' excitement grew.

   The villagers excitement grew.

Focus Trait: Ideas
Details That Don't Belong

Opinion: Yeh-Shen was lonely.
Details:
1. She has no time to play with other children.
2. Her one special friend was a fish.
3. Yeh-Shen lost her slipper.
Detail 3 does not belong. It does not support the opinion.

Read each opinion and the details that follow. Cross out the detail that does not support the opinion.

1. **Opinion:** Jin should not have cooked Yeh-Shen's
   fish friend.
   Details: The fish meant a lot to Yeh-Shen.
   Jin went to the pond and caught the fish.
   Yeh-Shen's friendship with the fish did not keep her
   from doing her work.

2. **Opinion:** It was good that Yeh-Shen followed the
   old man's advice.
   Details: A traveler found Yeh-Shen's slipper.
   Yeh-Shen's wish was granted.
   The bones of the fish had special powers.

3. **Opinion:** The king's treatment of Jin and Jun-li was
   too harsh.
   Details: Jin and Jun-Li could never come to the castle.
   Jin and Jun-Li had to stay in their cave.
   Jin and Jun-Li went to the festival.

Cumulative Review

Fill in the blanks.

Word Bank

bloom
crew
toss
yawn
shook

1. It rhymes with **moss**.
It begins like **took**. _____

2. It rhymes with **moo**.
It begins like **cross**. _____

3. It rhymes with **book**.
It begins like **show**. _____

4. It rhymes with **room**.
It begins likc **blue**. _____

5. It rhymes with **fawn**.
It begins like **yes**. _____

Now use words you wrote above to complete the sentences below.

6. Many flowers _____ in the spring.

7. A good _____ makes a ship
run smoothly.

8. When it got late, Tony started to _____.

Reader's Guide

Yeh-Shen

Write a Travel Brochure

Travelers want to take a tour and visit each place in Yeh-Shen's story. Tell why each place is important and draw a picture.

Read page 458.

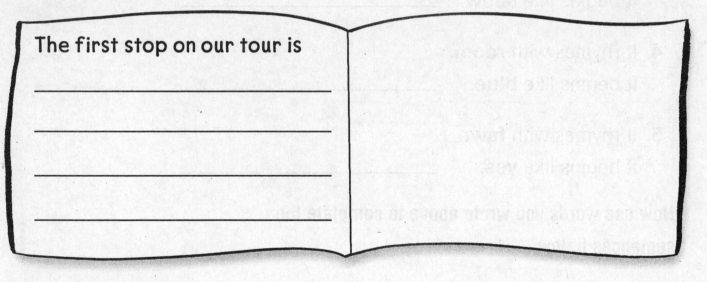

The first stop on our tour is

_____

_____

_____

_____

Read pages 459–460.

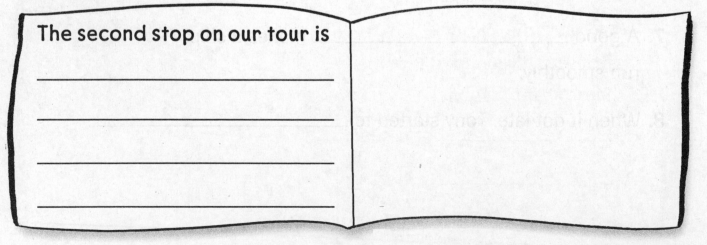

The second stop on our tour is

_____

_____

_____

_____

Read page 462–463.

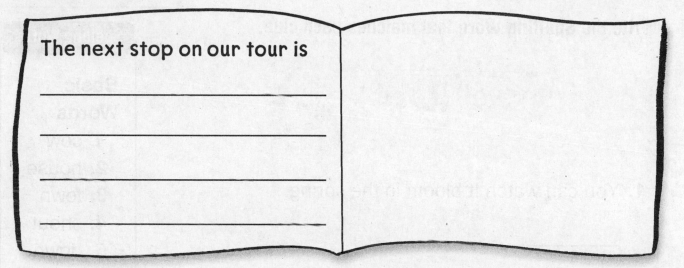

The next stop on our tour is

_____

_____

_____

_____

Read page 464.

The last stop on our tour is

_____

_____

_____

_____

Think about the whole story.

After this tour, many
visitors say they have learned
an important lesson:

_____

_____

_____

Words with *ow, ou*

Write the Spelling Word that matches each clue.

1. You can watch it bloom in the spring.

_____

2. When you call loudly, you

_____.

3. A _____ is smaller

than a city.

4. The opposite of *lost* is _____.

5. You may live in one of these.

_____

6. A noise that hurts your ears is _____.

7. This tiny animal is afraid of cats. _____

8. The opposite of *in* is _____.

9. You get milk from a _____.

10. The opposite of *up* is _____.

Basic Words
1. cow
2. house
3. town
4. shout
5. down
6. mouse
7. found
8. loud
9. brown
10. ground
11. pound
12. flower

Review Words
13. out
14. now

Possessive Nouns

✎ **Underline the sentence that uses a possessive noun correctly for nouns that name one.**

1. Her stepmother's demands were hard on Yeh-Shen.

Her stepmothers demands were hard on Yeh-Shen.

2. Yeh-Shen listened to the old mans advice.

Yeh-Shen listened to the old man's advice.

3. The girls wish came true.

The girl's wish came true.

4. The king's voice was full of kindness.

The kings voice was full of kindness.

✎ **Underline the sentence that uses a possessive noun correctly for nouns that name more than one.**

5. The slippers' size was very small.

The slippers size was very small.

6. The other girls' feet were too big.

The other girls feet were too big.

7. The soldiers job was hard.

The soldiers' job was hard.

8. The dancers movements were graceful.

The dancers' movements were graceful.

Classify and Categorize

Word Bank

prince	fairy godmother	stepsister
fish friend	king	girl
wise old man	traveler	

Read each word above. Write each word in the best category.

Characters in Fairy Tales	

Characters in Real Life	

Proofread for Spelling

Proofread the sentences. Circle the misspelled word. Then write the word correctly on the line.

Spelling Words

1. cow
2. house
3. town
4. shout
5. down
6. mouse
7. found
8. loud
9. brown
10. ground
11. pound
12. flower

1. When you see your present, you'll showt with joy!

_____

2. Is that a stuffed mowse? _____

3. I have never seen a flouwer shop like that one!

_____

4. That restaurant has the best waffles in toun.

_____

5. I have never seen her howse. _____

6. All of his clothes are broun. _____

7. It takes a good caw to make good milk.

_____

8. Come on doun to the kitchen for dinner!

_____

9. I fownd the book that I lost. _____

10. She dropped her sandwich on the grownd.

_____

Irregular Verbs

✏️ **Circle the word that correctly completes the sentence.**

1. Yeh-Shen (have, had) lots of chores.

2. She (do, did) her work well.

3. Yen-Shen (had, have) no help.

4. Jin and Jun-li (did, does) no work.

✏️ **Read the paragraph. Underline the six mistakes.**
Then rewrite the paragraph. Make sure each verb matches
the subject in the sentence.

   Long ago, Yeh-Shen have a hard life. Jin do mean
things to her. Yeh-Shen have only rags to wear. She do
chores all day. Then, Yeh-Shen have a wish. Her wish
came true and at last she do a happy life.

_____

_____

_____

_____

_____

Possessive Nouns

Weak	Strong
The slippers belonging to Yeh-Shen were silk.	Yeh-Shen's slippers were silk.
The advice of the old man was good.	The old man's advice was good.

Rewrite each sentence. Use a possessive noun to rewrite each underlined group of words. Write the new sentences on the line.

1. The eyes belonging to the fish were golden.

_____

2. The stepmother of Yeh-Shen was angry.

_____

3. Yeh-Shen followed the directions of the old man.

_____

4. The men of the king caught Yeh-Shen.

_____

Reading Longer Words: Long Vowels *a* and *i*

Write a word from the box to complete each sentence.

Word Bank

frightened	pasted	kindly
racecar	higher	explained

1. The _____ woman likes to

   help her neighbors.

2. Dale's _____ was speeding

   around the track.

3. Dad _____ the problem in a

   way I could understand.

4. Were you _____ by the

   strange sounds in the middle of the night?

5. We watched the hot air balloon rise

   _____ in the sky.

6. Gina _____ the photos into

   her scrapbook.

Pronouns and Ownership

- A **possessive pronoun** shows that a person or animal owns or has something.
- *My*, *your*, *his*, and *her* come before a noun to show that someone has or owns something.

My <u>mom</u> gets two gifts.

Thinking Question
What noun goes with the pronoun?

 Underline the possessive pronoun in each sentence. Circle the noun that goes with it.

1. His presents are on the table.

2. Mom also sees gifts from her children.

3. Her daughter gives two books.

4. Her son gives two flowers.

5. Mom opens your gifts, too.

6. My mom has a good birthday.

7. Her sister called this morning.

8. My dad will take her out to dinner tomorrow.

Name _____ Date _____

Lesson 29
READER'S NOTEBOOK

Two of Everything
Phonics: Reading Longer Words:
Long Vowels *a* and *i*

Reading Longer Words:
Long Vowels *a* and *i*

Read each clue. Choose the answer from the word pair below.

1. Doing something to have fun _____

Water coming down from the sky _____

raining   **playing**

2. Talk about things that trouble you _____

Tell what something means _____

explain   **complain**

3. Flashes of light during a storm _____

Above something else _____

lightning   **higher**

4. A track that trains run on _____

A thing that plays music _____

railway   **radio**

5. Bright and glowing _____

Moving through the sky with wings _____

flying   **shining**

Words with *ai, ay, igh, y*

Two of Everything
Spelling: Words with
ai, ay, igh, y

Sort the Spelling Words by the spelling patterns.

Spelling Words

Long *a* Sound

1. _____

2. _____

3. _____

4. _____

5. _____

6. _____

7. _____

8. _____

9. _____

Long *i* Sound

10. _____

11. _____

12. _____

13. _____

14. _____

Basic Words
1. aim
2. snail
3. bay
4. braid
5. ray
6. always
7. gain
8. sly
9. chain
10. shy
11. bright
12. fright

Review Words
13. tray
14. try

Underline the letters in each word that stand for the long *a* or long *i* sound.

Two of Everything
Grammar: Possessive Pronouns

More Pronouns and Ownership

- Some **possessive pronouns** stand alone. They are usually at the end of a sentence.
- *Mine*, *yours*, *his*, and *hers* are possessive pronouns.

Which <u>coins</u> are **yours**?

Thinking Question
Which word shows that someone has or owns something?

Underline the possessive pronoun. Circle the noun that shows what is owned.

1. The pennies are mine.

2. The dimes are hers.

3. The quarters are his.

4. The nickels are yours.

5. The money is mine.

6. Which bank is yours?

7. That wallet is his.

8. The purse is hers.

9. The dollar is mine.

10. The coins are yours.

Focus Trait: Ideas
Supporting Reasons

> Good writers tell their opinions in responses to literature.
> They give reasons for their opinions. They support their
> reasons with examples from the story.

**Read the opinion. Then read each reason that supports
the opinion. Find an example from *Two of Everything*
that supports each reason.**

Opinion: The pot makes the Haktaks happy.

Reason	Example
1. The pot makes them rich.	
2. The pot helps them get a lot of things they did not have before.	
3. The pot makes them new friends.	
4. The pot helps them make other things they need.	

Words with *oi, oy*

**Write the missing *oi* or *oy* word that will complete
each sentence.**

Word Bank

joined	voice	cowboy
noise	enjoyed	spoiled

1. The _____ sat by the campfire.

2. He had a very nice _____ for singing.

3. He _____ singing to pass the time.

4. Sometimes the cows _____ in.

5. Their mooing _____ his songs.

6. The lovely singing became frightful _____.

**Read each word you wrote above. Write each one in the
correct column below, under the word that has the same
vowel spelling.**

point	toy
_____	_____
_____	_____
_____	_____
_____	_____

Reader's Guide

Two of Everything

Make a Cartoon

Make a cartoon to tell the story of Mr. and Mrs. Haktak.
Draw characters and write what they say.

Read pages 488–489.

Read pages 490–492.

Read pages 496–497.

Read pages 501–502.

Words with *ai, ay, igh, y*

Write the Spelling Word that means the same as the given word.

Spelling Words

Basic Words
1. aim
2. snail
3. bay
4. braid
5. ray
6. always
7. gain
8. sly
9. chain
10. shy
11. bright
12. fright

Review Words
13. tray
14. try

1. get _____

2. forever _____

3. a scare _____

4. sneaky _____

5. point _____

6. shiny _____

Write the Spelling Word that belongs in each group.

7. plate, platter, _____

8. slug, worm, _____

9. pigtail, ponytail, _____

10. quiet, timid, _____

11. beam, light, _____

12. attempt, effort, _____

13. rope, leash, _____

14. sea, harbor, _____

Possessive Pronouns

Underline the possessive pronoun in each sentence.
Circle the noun that goes with it.

1. Dana and Dan are my pals.

2. The twins help you with your homework.

3. Her help is with math.

4. His help is with reading.

5. My friends like to help people.

Underline the possessive pronoun in each sentence.
Circle the noun that goes with it.

6. The skates are mine.

7. The hats are yours.

8. The bats are his.

9. The balls are hers.

10. The tickets are mine.

Name _____ Date _____

Lesson 29
READER'S NOTEBOOK

Two of Everything
Vocabulary Strategies:
Antonyms

Antonyms

Circle the antonyms in each sentence. Then write what each antonym means.

1. She put one purse into the pot and pulled out two.

   _____

2. They worked late filling and emptying the pot.

   _____

3. The branch swung high and low in the wind.

   _____

4. The tiny mouse wanted to be as huge as a horse.

   _____

5. The chair was heavy, but the pillows were light.

   _____

6. Mike was glad to have a rest, but Patty was unhappy.

   _____

7. Her dress was colorful, but her coat was faded.

   _____

Proofread for Spelling

**Proofread the paragraph. Circle the six misspelled words.
Then write the correct spellings on the lines below.**

I am alwas late getting ready for school. My
mother says I am the only girl who actually does move
as slowly as a snayl. I take a long time to brade my hair,
and I brush my teeth over and over until they are
brite. Each day, I aym to move more quickly, but it
never quite works out. When I get to school, I have to
explain why I am late to my teacher. That is hard for me
because I am shi.

Spelling Words

**Basic
Words**

1. aim
2. snail
3. bay
4. braid
5. ray
6. always
7. gain
8. sly
9. chain
10. shy
11. bright
12. fright

1. _____   4. _____

2. _____   5. _____

3. _____   6. _____

Unscramble the letters to write a Spelling Word.

7. yar   _____

8. lys   _____

9. nachi   _____

10. inag   _____

11. bya   _____

12. firght   _____

Irregular Verbs

✎ **Write each sentence. Use the past-tense verb.**

1. Yesterday, dogs (run, ran) through the park.

_____

2. Two birds (come, came) after them.

_____

3. They (go, went) to the lake.

_____

4. They (see, saw) a giant rainbow.

_____

✎ **Replace each underlined word with a word from the box. Write the new sentences.**

came	went	saw	ran

5. The boys <u>watched</u> two movies.

_____

6. They <u>walked</u> to two games.

_____

7. They <u>dashed</u> around the field.

_____

8. Then they <u>traveled</u> to my house.

_____

Possessive Pronouns

Weak	Strong
The teacher gave tests to the **teacher's** class.	The teacher gave tests to **her** class.
The student studied for the **student's** tests.	The student studied for **his** tests.

Rewrite each paragraph. Replace the underlined words with the possessive pronoun *mine, his, your,* **or** *her.*

Miss Lee gave two tests today. Miss Lee got papers from Miss Lee's drawer.

Miss Lee said to the students, "Take out the students' pencils."

Dave took out Dave's green pencil. Annette picked up my blue pencil. I said, "That is the one that belongs to me.

_____

_____

_____

_____

_____

_____

Reading Longer Words: Long *o* and *e*

Read the sentences. Draw a circle around each word that has the long *o* sound spelled *o, oa,* or *ow,* or the long *e* sound spelled *ee* or *ea*.

1. Rosa looked out the window on the coldest day of winter.

2. She noticed snowflakes floating down.

3. Slowly, the snow got deeper.

4. The snowplow went by on the street.

5. This might be the biggest snowstorm of the season.

Now write each word you circled under the word that has the same spelling for the same vowel sound.

folding	**blowing**	**freezing**
_____	_____	_____
_____	_____	_____
_____	_____	
	_____	
coasting	_____	**meaning**
_____	_____	_____

Adjectives and Adverbs

- **Adjectives** are words that tell more about nouns.

  Ben Franklin had many <u>remarkable</u> talents.

- **Adverbs** are words that tell more about verbs.

  He played the harmonica <u>beautifully</u>.

Thinking Question
What word does the adjective or adverb tell more about?

Write whether the underlined word in each sentence is an adjective or an adverb. Circle the word it tells more about.

1. Ben thought <u>creatively</u>. _____

2. Ben played an <u>important</u> role in developing America's Constitution.

   _____

3. He had many <u>wonderful</u> achievements. _____

4. His inventions <u>greatly</u> affect our lives today.

   _____

5. We <u>definitely</u> owe him our thanks. _____

Name _____ Date _____

Lesson 30
READER'S NOTEBOOK

Now & Ben
Phonics: Reading Longer Words:
Long Vowels o and e

Reading Longer Words: Long Vowels *o* and *e*

Fill in the blank.

Word Bank

reason
steepest
sweeter
homerun
notepad

1. We hiked up the hill on the

_____ trail.

2. Tracey hit a _____ to win

the game.

3. Do you have a good _____

for being late?

4. Make a list of things we need on the

_____.

5. Cupcakes are _____ than popcorn.

Read the words below. Think how the words in each group are alike. Write the missing word that will fit in each group.

Word Bank

loading
soapsuds
window
evening
leaving

6. morning, afternoon, _____

7. packing, filling, _____

8. door, wall, _____

9. moving away, going, _____

10. foam, bubbles, _____

Words with *oa, ow, ee, ea*

Now & Ben
Spelling: Words with
oa, ow, ee, ea

Sort the Spelling Words by the long *e* and long *o* vowel sounds.

Spelling Words

Long *e* Sound

1. _____
2. _____
3. _____
4. _____
5. _____
6. _____
7. _____

Long *o* Sound

8. _____
9. _____
10. _____
11. _____
12. _____
13. _____
14. _____

Basic Words

1. seated
2. keeps
3. speed
4. seen
5. means
6. clean
7. groan
8. roast
9. bowls
10. crow
11. owe
12. grown

Review Words

13. green
14. snow

Now sort the words by how the vowel sound is spelled.

Long *e* Spelled

ee	ea
15. _____	19. _____
16. _____	20. _____
17. _____	21. _____
18. _____	

Long *o* Spelled

oa	ow
22. _____	24. _____
23. _____	25. _____
	26. _____
	27. _____
	28. _____

Adjectives and Adverbs

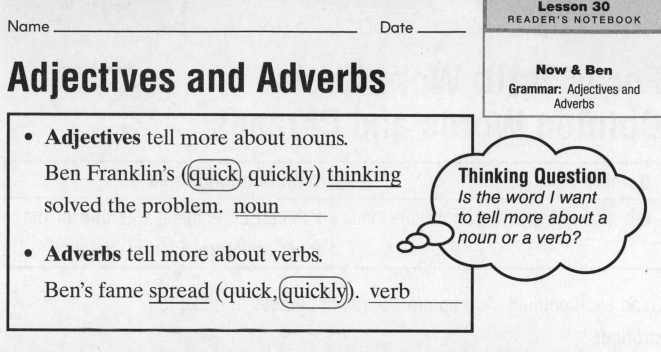

- **Adjectives** tell more about nouns.

  Ben Franklin's (quick, quickly) <u>thinking</u>
  solved the problem. <u>noun</u>

- **Adverbs** tell more about verbs.

  Ben's fame <u>spread</u> (quick, quickly). <u>verb</u>

> **Thinking Question**
> *Is the word I want to tell more about a noun or a verb?*

Write *noun* or *verb* to tell about the underlined word. Then circle
the adjective or adverb in ( ) to correctly complete the sentence.

1. Ben (strong, strongly) <u>promoted</u> the eating of citrus fruit.

_____

2. He believed eating fruit would prevent an (awful, awfully) <u>disease</u>.

_____

3. Ben created (beautiful, beautifully) <u>music</u>.

_____

4. His music (deep, deeply) <u>moved</u> many composers.

_____

5. Many people (great, greatly) <u>appreciated</u> Ben's achievements.

_____

Focus Trait: Word Choice
Opinion Words and Phrases

Opinion	With Opinion Words
Ben Franklin was an important man.	**I think** Ben Franklin was **one of the most important** men in history.

Read each opinion. Add opinion words or phrases to make it stronger.

Opinion	With Opinion Words
1. Ben Franklin was the greatest inventor.	
2. Ben Franklin's hospital made his city better.	
3. The documents that Ben Franklin helped to write were very important.	
4. Ben Franklin's work in the past is important for our future.	

Final Stable Syllable -*le*

Read the clues. Then write one of the two words below each clue in the blank.

1. A kind of dog _____

A horn for making music _____

beagle   **bugle**

2. A sweet, crunchy fruit _____

To eat in small bites _____

nibble   **apple**

3. Used for mending clothes _____

A soft food in some soups _____

noodle   **needle**

4. Easy to do _____

Peaceful or kind _____

gentle   **simple**

5. Burned to give light _____

A small pool of rainwater _____

candle   **puddle**

Reader's Guide

Now and Ben

Make a Drawing and Label It

Imagine that Ben Franklin made a time machine and traveled into our time. Make a sketch of some of his inventions that we still use. Write a sentence explaining to him how each invention has changed.

Read pages 528–529. Suppose Ben saw a swimmer practicing with flippers and fins.

	_____
	_____
	_____
	_____

Read pages 532. Suppose Ben saw a school with a desk and chair.

	_____
	_____
	_____
	_____

Read page 534. Suppose Ben saw an odometer on a car.

_____

_____

_____

Read page 535. Suppose Ben saw a library.

_____

_____

_____

Words with *oa, ow, ee, ea*

Write the Basic Word that matches each clue.

1. in a chair _____

2. large black bird _____

3. how fast you move _____

4. to cook in an oven _____

5. not dirty _____

6. a croaking or unhappy sound

_____

Write the Basic Word that completes each sentence.

7. Milk spilled when the cereal _____

   fell off the table.

8. I _____ my brother 25 cents.

9. When I am _____, I will be much

   taller.

10. I have never _____ an eagle.

Spelling Words

Basic Words
1. seated
2. keeps
3. speed
4. seen
5. means
6. clean
7. groan
8. roast
9. bowls
10. crow
11. owe
12. grown

Review Words
13. green
14. snow

Adjectives and Adverbs

- **Adjectives** are words that tell about nouns.
- **Adverbs** are words that tell about verbs.

Ben was a (careful, carefully) <u>swimmer</u>.

Ben <u>put on</u> the flippers (careful, carefully).

Write *noun* or *verb* to tell about the underlined word.
Then circle the adjective or adverb to correctly complete
each sentence.

1. Many people <u>admired</u> Ben (great, greatly).

_____

2. Ben <u>solved</u> problems (quick, quickly).

_____

3. Ben created (useful, usefully) <u>inventions</u>.

_____

4. Some of Ben's <u>work</u> was (dangerous, dangerously).

_____

5. Ben <u>shared</u> his inventions (eager, eagerly).

_____

Name _____ Date _____

Lesson 30
READER'S NOTEBOOK

Now & Ben
Vocabulary Strategies:
Root Words

Root Words

Underline the root word in each word. Use what you know about the root word to figure out the word's meaning. Complete each sentence by writing the word whose meaning fits best.

> **Vocabulary**
>
> western   toaster   reheat   strongest
> undone   writer   stinky   unearth

1. I tripped because my shoelaces were

_____.

2. "That dog is _____," said Ms.

Petersen. "She needs a bath."

3. Jose saw a beautiful rainbow in the

_____ sky.

4. A _____ told the class how she

gets ideas for her stories.

5. If we dig here, I bet we'll _____

a treasure.

6. "Please put my bread in the _____,"

said Sophie's father.

7. Hank is the _____ batter on the team.

He hit six homeruns.

8. The soup is cold, so we must _____ it.

Proofread for Spelling

Proofread the postcard. Circle the six misspelled words. Then write the correct spellings on the lines below.

Dear Tomas,

You would not believe the things we have sean on our trip. We went to a place where potters make clay boals big enough to sit in! Can you imagine being seeted in a pot? Each pattern meens something different. If a crowe is painted, it is for good luck. I hope the town keaps making the pottery so you can see it someday.

Manny

1. _____ 4. _____

2. _____ 5. _____

3. _____ 6. _____

Unscramble the letters to write a Spelling Word.

7. angro _____

8. weo _____

9. despe _____

10. leanc _____

11. stoar _____

12. rowng _____

Spelling Words

Basic Words
1. seated
2. keeps
3. speed
4. seen
5. means
6. clean
7. groan
8. roast
9. bowls
10. crow
11. owe
12. grown

Review Words
13. green
14. snow

Irregular Verbs

Underline the correct verb to finish each sentence.
Use the clue that tells when the action happens.

1. We (give, gave) reports today.   **Now**

2. I (take, took) the topic of Ben Franklin.   **Past**

3. Sara and I (eat, ate) lunch.   **Past**

4. The teacher (say, said) I could give my report first.   **Past**

Read this story about something that happened last
week. Write the underlined words correctly. Use verbs that
tell about the past.

    I <u>eat</u> lunch with my sister. She <u>give</u> me a library
book. It was about Ben Franklin. She <u>say</u> she liked it.
I <u>take</u> the book to my room. It was a good book. Ben
Franklin <u>give</u> the world many things. It <u>take</u> me just a
little while to read the book.

_____

_____

_____

_____

Adjectives and Adverbs

- **Adjectives** tell more about nouns.

  He heard the <u>loud</u> thunder.

- **Adverbs** tell more about verbs.

  He prepared his equipment <u>carefully</u>.

Write *noun* or *verb* to tell about the underlined word. Then circle the adjective or adverb in ( ) to correctly complete the sentence.

1. It <u>rained</u> (heavy, heavily).

_____

2. (Bright, Brightly) <u>lightning</u> lit up the sky.

_____

3. Ben Franklin had a (bold, boldly) <u>idea</u>.

_____

4. His <u>plan</u> was (dangerous, dangerously).

_____

5. His experiment <u>worked</u> (perfect, perfectly).

_____

Name _____ Date _____

Unit 6
READER'S NOTEBOOK

Exploring Space Travel
Segment 1
Independent Reading

Reader's Guide

Exploring Space Travel

Be an Astronaut!

Read page 12. Imagine you're an astronaut
on the Soyuz. The Soyuz has three modules.
Write notes that tell about each module.

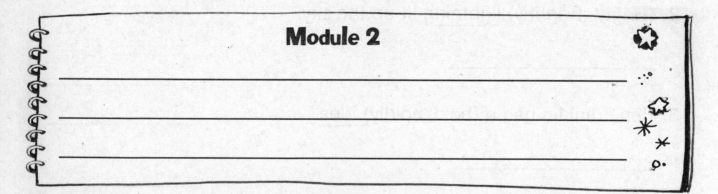

Module 1

_____

_____

_____

Module 2

_____

_____

_____

Module 3

_____

_____

_____

Name _____ Date _____

Unit 6
READER'S NOTEBOOK

Exploring Space Travel
Segment 1
Independent Reading

Use the picture on page 12 to help you draw a diagram of the Soyuz spacecraft. Then write the module numbers and use your notes to tell how the astronauts use each module. After you write, draw a line connecting the writing to each module.

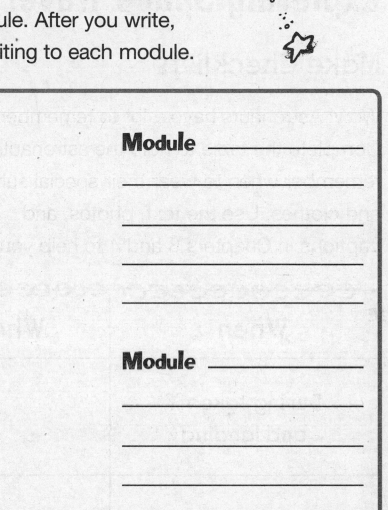

Module _____

_____

_____

_____

Module _____

_____

_____

_____

Module _____

_____

_____

_____

Reader's Guide

Exploring Space Travel

Make Checklists

Wow! Astronauts have a lot to remember. Complete the table to help the astronauts remember when to wear their special suits and clothes. Use the text, photos, and captions in Chapters 3 and 4 to help you.

When	What to Wear
During takeoff and landing	
On spacewalks	
In the spacecraft when working	

Name _____ Date _____

Unit 6
READER'S NOTEBOOK

Exploring Space Travel
Segment 2
Independent Reading

There is no gravity in the spacecraft. Objects and people are weightless. Make a checklist to remind astronauts how to stay safe without gravity. Add details to tell them why.

When	What to Do
Eating	
Sleeping	
Working	

Name _____ Date _____

Unit 6
READER'S NOTEBOOK

Exploring Space Travel
Segment 3
Independent Reading

Reader's Guide

Exploring Space Travel

Become an Astronaut!

Read pages 29–37. Think about what people
have to do so they can become astronauts.
Make a web that shows four things a person
must do to become an astronaut.

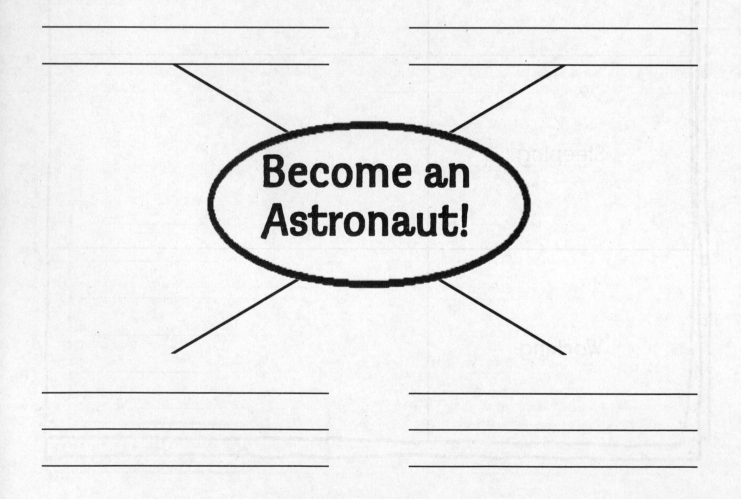

_____   _____
_____   _____
_____   _____

Become an Astronaut!

_____   _____
_____   _____

Look back at your web. Use those facts to make an ad that will tell people how to become an astronaut. Remember that an ad should be exciting to get people's attention.

Become an Astronaut!

_____

_____

_____

_____

_____